D1388214

Gallery Books
Editor: Peter Fallon

VOLUNTEERS

Brian Friel

VOLUNTEERS

Gallery Books

This edition of
Volunteers
is first published
simultaneously in paperback
and in a clothbound edition
in November 1989.

The Gallery Press
Loughcrew
Oldcastle
County Meath
Ireland

ISBN 1 85235 038 5 (*paperback*)
1 85235 039 3 (*clothbound*)

Volunteers was published first by Faber and Faber Limited in 1979.
All rights in this play are strictly reserved. Applications for profes-
sional and amateur productions should be addressed to Curtis Brown
Ltd., 162-168 Regent Street, London WIR 5TB.
  The Gallery Press receives financial assistance from An
Chomhairle Ealaíon / The Arts Council, Ireland, and acknowledges
also the assistance of the Arts Council of Northern Ireland in the
publication of this book.

for Seamus Heaney

Volunteers was first performed at the Abbey Theatre, Dublin, on 5 March 1975, with the following cast:

GEORGE	Edward Golden
MR WILSON	Peadar Lamb
KNOX	Micheál O Bríain
BUTT	Geoffrey Golden
SMILER	Niall O'Brien
KEENEY	Donal Donnelly
PYNE	Raymond Hardie
DESMOND	Bryan Murray

Direction	Robert Gillespie
Setting and costumes	Wendy Shea

Time and place

The present in Ireland, an archaeological site in the centre of the city.

The action takes place in a huge crater or, as KEENEY *describes it, 'a huge womb' or a 'prison yard'.*

The back wall is a fifteen-foot bank shored up by beams. On top of this bank, i.e. at street level, sheets of corrugated iron prevent sightseers from looking down into the pit. Above and beyond this protective fence we can see rooftops, TV aerials, etc. This bank is shelved at a height of seven feet. Along the back wall this shelf is perhaps two feet wide, anyhow wide enough for a man to walk along it.

Occupying a large portion of stage right (left and right from audience point of view) is the office which is built on this seven-foot-high shelf; in fact only a cross-section of this office — we have got to see inside it. Inside the office is a large drawing-table, shelves, wall-charts, etc., the usual site-works office.

A wooden verandah with a railing runs round this office. And one gets from the site-floor to the office level by a wooden stairway. On the verandah is a trestle-table.

The floor of the site, i.e. boulder clay level, is littered with planks, plastic bags, wheelbarrows, timbers on which the barrows run, etc. But the two dominant features on the boulder clay/stage floor level are the remains of a clay-and-wattle house and the skeleton, Leif.

The house — about twenty feet by fifteen feet — is really only a rectangular outline. The clay-and-wattle walls have crumbled away and are now only about five inches high. The house is left of stage centre.

The skeleton of Leif is right of stage centre. Although it lies on the flat, feet to the audience, it will have to be banked slightly so that it can be seen fully and clearly. The cesspit is off stage left. We see only the timbers supporting the wooden surround. There are two entrances: one left beside the pit; and one at back stage right. The entrance left leads past the cesspit (off) and to the tool-house (off) and the street above. The entrance back right leads to another area being excavated.

9

(Note to director: Throughout the play, especially in Act 1, there is a lot of archaeological business and the actors are constantly entering and exiting as they do this work. This will have to be worked into the script during rehearsals. The only business I have indicated and the only exit and enter directions I have scripted are those which are absolutely necessary.)

ACT ONE

Early in September. About 8.00 a.m. GEORGE *enters left. A bachelor of about fifty. Competent at his work and eminently reliable. Precise in manner and humourless in disposition. On a site he prefers to be associated with the academics than with the diggers. Under one arm his lunch-tin, under the other a large, brown paper parcel (the jug). He crosses the set, climbs up the stairs, unlocks the office door and enters. Hangs up his raincoat and cap. Lights the portable gas stove. Takes the wrapping off the jug, carries it outside and leaves it on the trestle-table. Returns to the office where he picks up a bucket and disappears behind the office. We hear the bucket being filled from a tap. Reappears and leaves the bucket beside the trestle-table. Goes into the office again and emerges with two cardboard shoe-boxes filled with pot-shards, bones, shells, etc. Throughout most of the morning he washes these finds in the water and stores them.*

Just before he begins this washing job someone off kicks three times on the corrugated paling.

GEORGE Come on! Come on! It's not locked!

> *After a brief delay, during which* GEORGE *goes on working,* WILSON *enters. A lean, tough, city-man in his sixties. Probably served in the British army as a young man. He is now in civilian clothes and looks — and probably feels — dressed up. During the* GEORGE/ WILSON *exchange we hear voices off occasionally.*

WILSON Good morning, George.
GEORGE Good morning, Mr. Wilson.
WILSON Touch of frost this morning.
GEORGE Season of mists and mellow fruitfulness.
WILSON What's that?
GEORGE The summer's gone, Mr. Wilson.
WILSON Well, we got our share.

GEORGE True enough and more than our share. (WILSON *yawns*) Tired?

WILSON Thank God it's Friday. The week on the early shift always kills me.

> WILSON *goes slowly up the steps, passing the time, whistling, looking around without interest.*

Funny, you get so used to looking at a place, you almost forget what it was like before you boys started hoking it up. That's where the car park ended there, didn't it?

GEORGE A bit further over.

WILSON And there were houses beyond that?

GEORGE That's right — above the paling.

WILSON Bloody marvellous.

GEORGE That's the way.

WILSON Hard to imagine a bloody big hotel standing here. I suppose that'll be the basement and kitchen and things down there.

GEORGE At the very bottom? I'm told that'll be a swimming pool.

WILSON Hoh! Very swanky.

GEORGE So they say.

WILSON Well, there can't be much left for you boys now, George?

GEORGE We're finished, Mr. Wilson.

WILSON Aye, another week'll see you through.

GEORGE This is our last day.

WILSON What?

GEORGE Packing up this evening.

WILSON You're not serious?

GEORGE Orders from the boss: no more digging after today.

WILSON The least he might have done was notify us.

GEORGE He'll be in touch with you this morning. The builders gave him an ultimatum last night — they won't hold off any longer.

WILSON That was bloody sudden.

GEORGE In a way. But the season's as good as over and we've got all we want anyway.

> *Laughter, off.*

WILSON   They don't know, do they?

GEORGE   Not yet.

WILSON   Will you tell them or will we?

GEORGE   Might be wiser not to mention it to them at all. They can be told some time over the weekend.

Another burst of laughter, off.

WILSON   That'll knock some of the spunk out of them. But to tell you the God's truth, George, I'll not be sorry. I'm sick trotting over and back twice a day.

GEORGE   I'm sure you are. But you certainly pulled us out of a hole, Mr. Wilson.

WILSON   Well, I mean to say —

GEORGE   No, no, only for you we couldn't have carried on.

WILSON   We did what we could.

GEORGE   Dr. King and I are most grateful; and I'm sure he's told you that many's the time.

WILSON   Oh, he has indeed. Fine man. Fine gentleman. (*Sees the jug on the table*) Hi-hi-hi what's this?

GEORGE   What?

WILSON   You have the lad all put together!

GEORGE   (*Pretending innocence*) Who?

WILSON   The yoke there!

GEORGE   Oh.

WILSON   By God, that was some job — eh?

GEORGE   Aye.

WILSON   You must be at him damn near three months.

GEORGE   Fourteen weeks and two days — not counting nights.

WILSON   I know; sure wasn't I here when the bits were got up in the corner. Butt came on them, didn't he?

GEORGE   It was Smiler actually — strange as it may seem.

WILSON   And how many pieces was there?

GEORGE   Five hundred and ninety-three as a matter of interest.

WILSON   (*Lifting the jug*) And you got them all fitted together!

GEORGE   A bit of a challenge all right. Easy, Mr. Wilson, easy!

WILSON   Only I seen it with my own eyes I wouldn't believe it.

GEORGE   A little patience — a little art — and there he is in all his pristine dignity.

WILSON   Bloody marvellous! He'll be worth a bob or two,

George?

GEORGE Money couldn't buy that.

WILSON That's a fact?

GEORGE Priceless, Mr. Wilson. A thing like that's beyond value.

WILSON My God. And he'll be a fair age, George?

GEORGE (*Taking jug*) Let's see . . . twelve inches high, green glaze, unpatterned except for gently fluted lip, French in style obviously . . . I would hazard . . . early thirteenth century.

WILSON My God — thirteenth century!

GEORGE Early thirteenth.

WILSON Tch-tch. Bloody shocking.

GEORGE But don't quote me on that. That's only an educated guess. Dr. King'll give us a precise dating.

WILSON Bloody desperate.

GEORGE Funny thing, the layman always finds it fascinating. To us it's just another job of work — you know.

Another burst of mocking laughter, off.

They seem in good form.

WILSON Bloody trash. (GEORGE *laughs*) Amn't I right? How would you describe them?

GEORGE I wouldn't quarrel with that.

WILSON 'Political prisoners' — huh! In my book they're all bloody criminals. And now that this job's over, that's what they'll miss most — you know — the chance to talk. Would you believe it, George, since the day they volunteered to work here five months ago — May 3, am I right?

GEORGE Correct.

WILSON Not one of their mates back there has broken breath with them.

GEORGE I know. You've told me.

WILSON Not one. What about that for solidarity?

GEORGE Remarkable.

WILSON And outside it's the same thing — they're a dirty word with their mates outside, too. Mind you, George, I'm not bleeding for them. Matter of fact it suits us down to the ground: run away from here and their own crowd would get them before we could reach them.

GEORGE They're nicely cornered.

WILSON Cornered's the word. Not a friend inside or out. But to be sent to Coventry for three months — believe me, George, that's bloody tough.

GEORGE They're tough men, Mr. Wilson.

WILSON You've got to be hard to survive that.

GEORGE All the same they performed a public service — not that they'll see it that way.

WILSON Damn right, they won't.

GEORGE And maybe we expanded their horizons just a little, too.

WILSON Huh!

GEORGE You never know these things, Mr. Wilson.

WILSON Don't fool yourself. No, no, George, speaking from a lifetime of practical experience, you're either born right or you're not. And there's nothing nor nobody can change the way you were born. I'm a firm believer in genetics and in all my years in the service I've never seen —

> *He breaks off because* KNOX *has entered.* KNOX *— a snuffling, shuffling, grubby man of about sixty-five but looks older. Because of his very thick glasses he thrusts his face right up to people when he is speaking to them. Not far removed from the kind of man one sees at night wrapped in newspapers and sleeping in the doorways of banks and cinemas.*
>
> *As he enters, KNOX is pulling on dungarees and carrying wellingtons — the outfit all the diggers wear. He walks with the slow, sleepy movements of early-morning workmen.*

Well, just take my word for it, George.

GEORGE Morning, Knox.

> *No answer.*

WILSON Didn't you hear George speaking to you?

> KNOX *looks up, grunts something inaudible and*

shuffles across the stage.

Bloody pig. One of these days I'll expand his backside with my bloody boot.

GEORGE Are you not working today?

WILSON Got a couple of hours off.

> *Enter* BUTT *and* SMILER. BUTT *is a countryman in his late forties. A quiet man who gives an impression of strength and obstinacy and self-knowledge.*
>
> SMILER *is about thirty-five. There is no trace of the man* SMILER *once was. We see only the imbecile with the perpetual grin. He wears a woollen ski-cap with a huge tassel that looks suitably ridiculous in this context.*
>
> *Both men are adjusting their clothes as they enter.*

GEORGE Yes, men.

BUTT Yes, George.

GEORGE How are you, Smiler?

SMILER That's right — that's right.

WILSON Go on, Smiler, go on — get started. (*Lowering his voice; to* GEORGE) As a matter of fact, I'm bringing the eldest girl, Dolly, to her music examination.

> *Mocking laughter, off.*

GEORGE Ah.

WILSON Grade Four. Guildhall School of Music, London. Practical.

GEORGE Pianoforte?

WILSON Viola.

GEORGE Viola? Very nice.

WILSON The viola's a nice instrument.

GEORGE Lovely instrument, the viola.

WILSON Nice for a girl. You know — mellow.

GEORGE Lovely for a girl.

WILSON Takes it from her mother's side — sodden with music.

GEORGE There you are — proves your point.

WILSON What's that?

GEORGE It's in the blood. Genetics.

WILSON You see!

GEORGE Well, I hope she does great.

WILSON (*Descending briskly*) Thanks, George. I'll be able to tell you all this evening.

> *He is the prison officer again. Looks off-stage where he sees* KEENEY *and* PYNE *approaching.*

Right, then — everybody accounted for? Come on, you two! One — two — three — four — five. All present and correct. Over to you now, George.

GEORGE Over and out, Mr. Wilson.

> *The moment* WILSON *leaves,* KEENEY *and* PYNE *enter and at the same moment burst into their usual excessively enthusiastic greeting. No one pays the least attention to them.* KEENEY *is in his forties. Quick-witted, quick-tongued, and never for a second unaware. Years of practice have made the public mask of the joker almost perfect.*
>
> PYNE *is more than ten years younger than* KEENEY, *but an eager apprentice. He is now so attuned to* KEENEY *that his harmonies to* KEENEY'S *themes are expert. But unlike* KEENEY *his public mask slips in times of crisis. His is the uncertain breeziness of a sailor. They move about the stage, waving, smiling, pouring out their double-act patter at great speed.*

KEENEY Good morning, George! (*Calls*) Good morning, Leif! Morning, Knox. Morning, Butt. Morning, Smiler. (*Calls*) Hello, Leif!

PYNE (*At the same time as* KEENEY *above*) Hello, George. (*Calls*) Hello Leif! Morning, Butt. Yes, Smiler. Hello, Knoxie. (*Calls*) Yes, Leif!

KEENEY Morning, George.

PYNE Morning, George.

KEENEY One political limerick coming up, George. Composed in the monastic silence of last night.

PYNE Hear ye! Hear ye!

KEENEY There once was a bird called O'Shea
Who was known as a fabulous lay.
PYNE Yea-yea.
KEENEY Then along came Parnell
Who screwed her to hell
And we feel the results to this day.
PYNE Wheee!

KEENEY *goes straight into an exaggerated military march.*

KEENEY Hup: One — two — three — four.
Hup: One — two — three — four.

As soon as KEENEY *begins to march* PYNE *falls in behind him. Their wellington boots make the march ridiculous.*

PYNE (*Now marching*) God bless you, men. You're doing a splendid job.
KEENEY (*Marching rhythm*) Your granny was there when you left.
PYNE You're right.
KEENEY With lots of gold hair on her chest.
PYNE You're right.
KEENEY Okay, Pyne. Your turn.
PYNE (*Saluting*) One limerick on the way, sir.

They stop marching. KEENEY *claps.*

KEENEY Thank you — thank you — thank you. You're a truly wunnerful people. And now, friends, I give you — Brother Pyne! Alleluia!
PYNE I've forgotten the first line.
KEENEY There once was a Norseman called Leif.
PYNE Got it. There once was a Norseman called Leif
Whose visit to Ireland was brief
He was caught in a war
Between Jesus and Thor
And came to a permanent grief.

KEENEY (*Clapping*) Wunnerful — wunnerful — wunnerful.

PYNE (*Bowing*) Thank you. Thank you.

KEENEY (*Rolling a cigarette*) Morning, George.

PYNE Yes, George.

KEENEY Nothing like beginning the day with a laugh, George, eh?

PYNE He won't answer us, Keeney.

KEENEY Could he be off-colour?

PYNE Are you off-colour, George?

KEENEY No, he's looking fine.

PYNE Handsome, too.

KEENEY D'you think so?

PYNE Very attractive.

KEENEY He thinks you're handsome, George. I'd watch that — never sure with these merchant seamen. (*To* PYNE) I thought you were married?

PYNE That's long over.

KEENEY English, wasn't she?

PYNE Once upon a time.

KEENEY Thought so. And now you fancy him?

PYNE George?

KEENEY He fancies you, George.

PYNE You're embarrassing him.

KEENEY George? Stalwart George? Never embarrass George. All the same I think he's *genuinely* glad to see us.

PYNE He ought to be. We're his trusted team.

KEENEY His researchers.

PYNE His right arm.

KEENEY His muscle and sinew.

PYNE And he's our foreman.

KEENEY George? George's more than a foreman.

PYNE Really?

KEENEY An expert in his own right, George. Worked with Dr. King on every major archaeological site in the country.

PYNE Go on!

KEENEY A craftsman to the soles of his feet, George.

PYNE You'd know by the look of him.

KEENEY Dr. King's right-hand man. Dedicated his last book to him.

PYNE Never!

KEENEY 'For George — my confrère.'

PYNE Beautiful.

KEENEY Shows what he thinks of him.

PYNE The world, I'd say.

KEENEY 'Confrère' — nice democratic touch, that.

PYNE God, that's moving.

KEENEY Only one snag, Pyne.

PYNE What's that?

KEENEY King's a quack.

PYNE D'you hear what he's saying?

KEENEY I'm afraid.

PYNE Quack! How could he be a quack! He's a doctor and a university professor!

KEENEY Quack-quack-quack-quack-quack.

PYNE Nothing but disappointments.

KEENEY And to disillusion you still further, friend, the book — like all his others — is shite.

PYNE Professor King's?

KEENEY S-h-i-g-h-t.

PYNE *laughs.*

PYNE What's it about?

KEENEY Establishing the age of an object by radiocarbon tests.

PYNE Has it a title?

KEENEY Tell him what it's called, George.

PYNE I'm telling you — he's huffing.

KEENEY It's called *Radiocarbon Dating in West Cork.*

PYNE Jesus!

KEENEY Put that in your dudeen.

PYNE In West Cork! So it has crept in there, too?

KEENEY The very dogs are at it in their sleep, man.

PYNE Agh, the country's finished.

KEENEY A randy young buck from Kilgarvan
On a girl tried out radiocarbon.

PYNE Yerra schtop, bhoy!

KEENEY Though she screamed as if thrilled

PYNE *gives girlish scream.*

The poor lad was chilled
To discover she dated pre-Norman.

PYNE Ha-ha.

KEENEY A *very* good morning to you, George.

KNOX Ground's bloody frozen. Couldn't work with ground like that.

PYNE A truer word was never spoke, Knoxie.

KNOX Give us a drag, Keeney. I'm out till Des comes.

KEENEY *gives him the cigarette he is smoking.*

Decent man.

He sucks greedily at the cigarette PYNE *goes over to* SMILER *and shadowboxes before him.*

PYNE Okay, Smiler?

SMILER Yes, Pyne.

PYNE I was watching you wolfing down a big bowl of porridge this morning.

SMILER That's right — that's right.

PYNE Great for keeping your mind off women — plenty of porridge and plenty of exercise; so the chaplain told me. (*Boxing*) One-two, one-two, bang, bang, bang.

He goes off. KNOX *offers the cigarette back to* KEENEY.

KNOX Ta. Here.

KEENEY After you've soaked it? D'you want me to get gangrene?

KNOX Bugger off.

KEENEY Language! Language! A very good morning to *you*, George.

GEORGE (*Dryly*) How are you, Keeney?

KEENEY (*Excessively*) Splendid, George, splendid. Thank you for asking. (*He bounds up the steps*) Senses vibrant, faculties alert, mind finely honed. And I've a feeling, George, I'm going to make a discovery of moment today.

KEENEY *slips past* GEORGE *and into the office. There he*

quickly gathers up cigarette butts from ashtrays. His
eyes dart around for anything else he might forage.
GEORGE *follows him into the office.*

GEORGE Come on, Keeney. Out of there.
KEENEY Just tidying up, George. An instinct you'd applaud.
GEORGE Out! Out!

KEENEY *puts the butts into a tin box.*

KEENEY Thank God Professor King smokes. Positive lifesaver
these. May the giving hand never fail. Pity he isn't an
alcoholic — with a harem.
GEORGE Out! Out! Out!
KEENEY True as God, George, at this very minute I'd give an arm
for a large, neat whiskey and a large, loose woman.
(*Discovery*) And a forgotten biscuit by the hokey! I told
you the discoveries would be momentous today.

Both KEENEY *and* GEORGE *are now out on the terrace.*

GEORGE You're here to work, Keeney.
KEENEY Tell me, George, in your considered opinion — an
educated guess, as you would put it —
GEORGE What?
KEENEY Was Hamlet really mad?
GEORGE Get down and get at it.

GEORGE *goes back to his table.* KEENEY *stays on the*
verandah, salvaging the tobacco from the butts.

BUTT Hi, Knox!
KNOX Wha'?
BUTT You have my wellingtons.
KNOX What d'you mean?
BUTT These are yours.
KNOX How d'you know?
BUTT Take them off. Take them off.

KEENEY *on the verandah wolf-whistles and claps.*

KEENEY Take them off, Knoxie! Take them off!

> BUTT *holding* KNOX's *boots at arms length and sniffing.*

BUTT 'How do you know?' he says.
KNOX Christ, you'd think he owned them.

> BUTT *cautiously runs his hand over the crumbling remains of the Viking house.*

BUTT Every day another bit crumbles away. And with this frost the ground's getting wetter and the whole damn thing's going to be lost. (*To* GEORGE) Did you ask him to get some scaffolding and a bit of canvas covering?
GEORGE Hardly worth our while now.
BUTT There's at least a week's work in this section alone.
GEORGE The budget's long spent.
BUTT Then we'll just have to cover the house and all this part with sacking. That might save it a bit.

> PYNE *enters with two buckets.*

PYNE You're a real dandy in that cap, Smiler.
SMILER That's right — that's right.
PYNE A real smasher, isn't he?
SMILER I got a new cap, George.
PYNE What d'you think of that for a cap, George?
GEORGE That's a nice cap, Smiler.
SMILER Butt gave it to me. Yes, Butt?
BUTT Yes, Smiler.
SMILER That's right. Butt gave it to me. And I stood up at the meeting and put the proposition to the house and at least half the delegates there were in favour but the crowd at the back began to heckle and . . .
BUTT (*Quietly, firmly*) That'll do for you.
SMILER . . . and the chairman called for a vote but no one was listening anymore and . . .
BUTT (*Stern command*) Shut up, Smiler! Just shut up!

> The others look away — they have witnessed this

23

before. SMILER's *brief elation dies; the vacuous smile returns. Pause.*

Now let's get some work done about here. The ground's not as hard in there in the shelter of the bank. So you take this section here, Knoxie, inside the house. Start at the door and work slowly up. And be careful close to the walls or they'll come away in your hands. I'll finish off outside the house. Smiler, you carry on along that street — but don't stand on the baulks. Pyne, you can finish that far section. Keeney, you . . . Keeney!

KEENEY My child.

BUTT Come on, Keeney.

KEENEY In nomine Smiler simplissimo et Knoxie stinkissimo et George industrissimo et —

BUTT There's work to be done.

KEENEY I'm on my holidays in Castel Gandolfo. Hi, Pyne!

PYNE What?

KEENEY You know those newsreels you see of the Pope being carried about through the thousands of tourists; well, d'you know what he's saying out of the corner of his mouth as he's making this gesture? (*He illustrates the arm gesture*)

PYNE I give up. What is he saying?

KEENEY 'Getta those wops offa de grass.'

PYNE Ha-ha.

BUTT Your turn for the cesspit, Keeney. The gloves and leggings are out at the far wall.

KEENEY *comes running down the steps.*

KEENEY Come on, Butt; fair's fair. I did the cesspit yesterday.

BUTT I did the cesspit yesterday. And Smiler did it on Wednesday. And Knox on Tuesday. And Pyne on Monday.

KEENEY Knoxie — be a sport.

KNOX Wha'?

KEENEY Do the pit and I'll give you three fags.

KNOX Bugger off!

KEENEY Five fags — handmade — monogrammed.

KNOX *gestures with his fingers and shuffles away.*

And the tragedy is the cesspit's a natural environment for a man like you. (*He looks around for another victim — everyone is now working. Only* SMILER *hasn't begun yet*) Smiler — Smiler — look, Smiler, look. (*He holds out two closed fists before* SMILER'S *face*) Chance of a lifetime. Toss you for the cesspit — okay?

SMILER Yes, Keeney.

BUTT Leave Smiler alone.

KEENEY Now, Smiler, which hand has a biscuit in it?

SMILER Which hand has a biscuit in it.

KEENEY No, no, there's a biscuit in one hand.

SMILER A biscuit.

KEENEY And if you pick the hand that has the biscuit you don't have to do the cesspit *and* you get the biscuit to keep! You understand?

SMILER Yes, Keeney.

KEENEY Good. Guess. Which hand?

SMILER That's right — that's right.

KEENEY *opens his right hand — it's empty.*

KEENEY No. It's the left. Hard luck, Smiler. A great effort. On with the leggings and away you go. Pull that cap down over your nose and you'll smell nothing. (*As* SMILER *leaves*) And if you find a crock of gold down there, I'll go halves with you. That's a promise — hold me to it.

PYNE Ha-ha.

BUTT Bastard!

KEENEY That's right, Buttie; that's right.

BUTT I'll not forget that, Keeney.

KEENEY Don't I know? That old Gaelic head's stocked with a million grudges. God bless it and God bless Ireland. (*Switching to sudden and very real concern*) Hi, boys, where's Leif?

PYNE Leif?

KEENEY Leif's gone.

PYNE Don't be silly.

KEENEY (*Calls*) Leif!

PYNE How could he be gone! He was here a minute ago.

They both begin moving around the stage looking for Leif. Nobody pays the slightest attention to them.

KEENEY I'm telling you — he's gone.
PYNE How can he be gone for God's sake!
KEENEY (*Calls*) Leeeif!
PYNE He must be here. He gave his word of honour to George, to Wilson, to all of us.
KEENEY He's gone — I'm telling you!
PYNE Good gracious! Don't stand there, men! Look for him! Look for him!
KEENEY Leif! Leif! Give us a hand, Butt. Come on, Knoxie, come on.
PYNE Leeeeeif!

KEENEY *races up the steps. As he passes* GEORGE:

KEENEY You'd better call his embassy. There could be an international incident over this. Leif! Leif!

KEENEY *takes a quick look into the office and runs down the stairs again. As he and* PYNE *pass:*

PYNE Maybe he just nipped out for a jar.
KEENEY Don't be ridiculous — he's been off it for centuries. Leeeif!

PYNE *rushes off calling Leif's name.*

KEENEY (*To* KNOX, *who ignores him*) Give his description to anyone you meet. Small, thin, very thin, leather thong around his neck, pronounced Scandinavian accent. Leeeif! (*To* BUTT, *who also ignores him*) And as Pyne says, he gave us all his word! You can trust no one these days.

He goes to the rectangular square of tarpaulin which is stretched on the ground just right of the house. Lifts up a corner and peeps under.

Aha, aha, aha.

PYNE (*Off*) Leif! Leif!

KEENEY (*Calls*) He's here, Pyne.

PYNE (*Off*) Where?

KEENEY (*To Leif*) You rascal.

PYNE *enters.*

PYNE God, that's a relief. Where is he?

KEENEY Here.

PYNE And he was hiding there all the time!

KEENEY (*Wagging his finger*) Naughty — naughty — naughty.

PYNE And wouldn't even answer you! I see no fun in that! Show me.

KEENEY Look — all innocence.

PYNE You divil you, Leif. You put the heart across us.

KEENEY You're a persistent joker, too, aren't you? All right, men, the panic's over. Back to work. All's well.

PYNE I was thinking he hadn't slipped out for a jar. I just said that for a laugh. (*He crouches down and peers under the tarpaulin*) Hi, Keeney, is he all right?

KEENEY Of course he's all right.

PYNE He's not looking well.

KEENEY I see no change.

PYNE Definitely lost weight.

KEENEY Maybe a pound or two.

PYNE What do you say, Butt?

KEENEY Here — take an end of this. That's it.

> *Together they remove the tarpaulin. And now for the first time we see Leif — a skeleton. The ground around him has all been scraped away, so that he is lying on top of the boulder clay. A leather rope hangs loosely round the neck. There is a small round hole in the skull.*

PYNE I'm telling you — I don't like the appearance at all. He'd just be skin and bone — if he had any skin. Okay,

Keeney — you found him — you're on it now. Give us ten to get away. (*As he runs off*) One — two — three — four — five — six — seven — (*Counting fades.* KEENEY *crouches down bedside Leif*)

KEENEY Nice wee hole that in the top of the head. I wonder what did it? Maybe an aul' pick-axe. Lovely bit of leather that, too, isn't it? Best of good stuff. And beautifully plaited. Man, that wouldn't chaff your neck at all. But the question persists, George — and who knows better than a metaphysician like yourself — damnit the question that haunts me, George, is: What in the name of God happened to him? D'you think now could he have done it to himself? Eh? Or maybe a case of unrequited love, George — what about that? Or maybe he had a bad day at the dogs? Or was the poor eejit just grabbed out of a crowd one spring morning and a noose tightened round his neck so that obeisance would be made to some silly god. Or — and the alternative is even more fascinating, George — maybe the poor hoor considered it an honour to die — maybe he volunteered: Take this neck, this life, for the god or the cause or whatever. Of course acceptance of either hypothesis would indicate that he was — to coin a phrase — a victim of his society. Now, you're an erudite man, Knoxie — what's your opinion?

KNOX Why don't you shut up, Keeney?

KEENEY Knoxie may well be on to something. Maybe he was a casualty of language. Damnit, George, which of us here isn't? But we're still left with the problem: Was Hamlet really mad?

PYNE (*Entering*) Are you playing or are you not?

KEENEY I'm always playing. Right, George? No, George and I were considering the hazards of language. (*Picks up a bucket and trowel. To Leif*) Don't stir till I come back.

PYNE And me out in the shed like a fool hiding behind the boss's anorak. (*To* GEORGE) Is he not coming in today?

KEENEY *looks as if he is about to begin working. He goes into the Viking house where* KNOX *is scraping, surveys the task, and lights a cigarette.*

KEENEY (*To* KNOX) God bless all here. And God bless you, man of the house.

PYNE George!

GEORGE What?

PYNE Is the boss not coming in today?

GEORGE He's at a meeting.

PYNE Great. And us slaving away here. And what the hell's keeping Dessy the Red? Is he not coming either?

GEORGE As far as I know he is.

PYNE These commies are all the same: grand for spouting revolution but not so good at doing an honest day's work.

> KEENEY *addresses* KNOX *very softly, very confidentially.*

KEENEY Desmond'll be late this morning.

KNOX Watch.

KEENEY Must be feeling terrible.

KNOX Get out of my road.

KEENEY Imagine having your stomach pumped for forty-five minutes. God — agony!

> PYNE, *sensing a game, joins the* KNOX/KEENEY *huddle.*

PYNE Was it really forty-five minutes?

KEENEY According to Wilson.

PYNE Jesus!

KNOX What are you ranting about now?

PYNE You're really going soft in the head, Knoxie! Didn't you hear Wilson telling us on the way over?

KEENEY No, Knoxie didn't hear. He was at the back of the van.

PYNE He must have.

KEENEY I'm telling you he didn't. He was at the back with Smiler.

KNOX Hear what? I didn't hear nothing about —

KEENEY Shhh! George isn't to know.

PYNE He'd tell the boss.

KNOX What about his stomach?

KEENEY Tell you later.

KNOX (*To* PYNE) Is Des sick?

KEENEY Later.

PYNE (*To* KEENEY) Go on — tell him. Knoxie can keep a secret.

KEENEY *looks cautiously around and then moves close to* KNOX.

KEENEY D'you remember a fortnight ago he got a telegram here that his Auntie Coco had died in California?

KNOX Aye, I —

PYNE Shhh!

KEENEY Well, they had her cremated out there and sent the remains back here. And when Des went back to his flat yesterday evening there was the casket.

PYNE Poor old Des.

KEENEY But there was no covering letter. And poor Desmond made a terrible mistake.

KEENEY *lights a cigarette and gives it to* KNOX.

KNOX Ta.

KEENEY He thought it was a swanky jar of American coffee and he made a cup of coffee out of his Auntie Coco.

PYNE (*Anguished*) O God!

KNOX You're a . . . !

KEENEY Of course the *moment* he realized, he rushed to the hospital and got it pumped out.

PYNE All of it?

KEENEY The very last grain.

PYNE That itself.

KEENEY But the pain of the stomach-pump — I'm told it's hell.

PYNE I can imagine.

KNOX You must take me for a bloody eejit!

KEENEY You, Knoxie? Never!

PYNE Shh! Here he is.

KEENEY But the really disquieting thing is this: Wilson says he *loved* the taste. Shh. Not a word.

DES *enters and* KEENEY *gets to his feet.* KNOX *stares at* DES. DES, *a student of archaeology. An earnest young man of about twenty. Carrying a shoulder bag.*

Ah! The coxcomb himself. (*Softly to* KNOX) Look at the bags under his eyes.

DES Morning, morning, morning.

GEORGE⎫
  BUTT⎰Good morning, Des.

DES God, it's nippy. Hard at it, Keeney?

KEENEY As usual, Desmond.

DES There's a pool of water gathered at that far foundation trench. Needs to be let away. (*To* PYNE) Take these up to the office, Pyne, would you? (*Hands* PYNE *a small parcel*) Thanks. Okay, gather round — gather round, gather round — who ordered what?

They gather round him as he produces things from his shoulder bag.

Last night's paper — anybody want it?

KEENEY I'll take it. (KEENEY *goes over to stage left and reads the paper*)

DES Razorblades — these are yours, Butt, aren't they?

BUTT Mine.

DES And your change.

BUTT Thanks.

DES (*Producing a magazine*) And that's the article you were asking about — establishing dates from the pattern of tree rings.

BUTT Good man.

DES There's another piece in that issue, too — actually we're mentioned in a footnote — about climatic conditions and the shells of *Mollusca*.

KEENEY (*Looking at the paper; almost to himself*) Many's the shell I took off Mollusca in my day.

DES A bit technical but worth persevering with.

KEENEY (*Still privately*) That describes her!

DES What are you muttering about, Keeney?

KEENEY (*Beaming*) Just trying to keep sane, Desmond.

DES Your chewing gum. (*He throws the packet to* KEENEY)

KEENEY Bless you.

BUTT Can I hold on to this (*magazine*) over the weekend?

DES Okay. But I'll want it back by Monday or Tuesday.

BUTT Thanks.

KEENEY (*Eyes still on his paper, again almost to himself*)
An assiduous old digger called Butt
Was disturbed with his life in a rut.

DES Was there anything else?

KNOX Ten fags for me.

DES Ten fags — here you are.

KEENEY I may be a conjunction
But I know it's my function
To inform my poor ignorant nut.
(*He senses* BUTT *staring aggressively at him. With a brilliant smile*) Splendid journal that, Buttie. Very scholarly.

KNOX (*To* DES) That's the wrong kind.

DES That's all they had in tens.

KNOX These are the dear ones.

DES Do you want them or do you not? (*To* PYNE *who is coming down the steps*) Your writing paper and envelopes.

PYNE Great. Thanks.

DES That's everything. No — you (KNOX) owe me a penny.

KNOX I — ?

DES You gave me 16p.

KNOX I gave you —

DES 16p and the fags cost 17.

KNOX These do!

DES One penny please.

KNOX Christ, he's making a fortune on us, all right!

DES I have to earn my fees somehow, don't I? (*Accepts the penny*) Thank you. And what the hell are you staring at?

KNOX Me? I'm not staring.

PYNE Of course you are. Leave poor Des alone. Des's fine now.

DES And if there's any more questioning about the orders, you can all get George to do your huckstering for you from now on.

GEORGE For that gang? Huh!

BUTT Des, you'll have to speak to the boss about getting some sort of covering for these last few weeks.

DES Why don't you ask him yourself?

BUTT Look at these posts. (*He points to the clay-and-wattle house*) The frost's playing hell with them. And the ground — another night like last night and you'd need a bloody drill. And if it rains on top of this, we'd be up to our knees in mud and we'd wreck all round us.

DES He'd listen to you quicker than he'd listen to me.

BUTT I'm a bloody labourer here.

DES And I'm a bloody student and he's my bloody professor! Okay, okay, I'll ask him again. Not that he gives a damn at this stage; he's got all he wants out of here and out of all of us. (*To* PYNE) Give me that spade — I want to clear that water.

PYNE (*Passing the spade*) I say he's lost a couple of pounds weight, Des. What d'you think?

DES Who?

PYNE Leif.

DES For God's sake, Pyne — it's too early in the morning.

PYNE Ha-ha.

DES *goes off.* KEENEY *leans over the cesspit.*

KEENEY Hello, hello, hello — is that you, Smiler? Speak up — the line's bad. Hello? Hello? Press button A, Smiler.

SMILER (*Off*) Yes, Keeney.

KEENEY That's better. Chewing gum — catch. (*He drops the packet down the pit*) Everything in hand down there?

SMILER (*Off*) That's right — that's right.

KEENEY (*To himself* That's right — that's right. Did you turn left? — That's right. Two and two make five — that's right. One little piggy was left — that's right. Oh my God.

BUTT Are you going to work or are you not?

KEENEY (*Charming*) How do you want to use my talents, bwana?

BUTT Do the street and do it carefully.

KEENEY Don't I always?

BUTT And watch where you're bloody-well walking.

KEENEY *gets down on his knees. And now for the first*

time all four diggers — BUTT, KNOX, PYNE *and* KEENEY
— are working.

    PYNE *whistles the opening bar of 'The Bonny
Labouring Boy' and then*:

PYNE (*Sings*)   As I went out one morning fair
                  All in the bloomin' spring
                  I overheard a damsel fair
                  Most grievously did sing:
                  'Cruel were my parents,
                  They did me sore annoy,
                  They would not let me tarry with
                  My bonny labouring boy'.
    (*He continues whistling*)

KNOX Did any of yous hear anything last night?

PYNE Hear what?

KNOX Noises.

PYNE Noises! What sort of noises?

KNOX Sounded like . . . (*dry chuckle*) . . . screaming?

    BUTT *stops working.*

PYNE When was this?

KNOX When? How would I know when? Some time in the middle of the night.

PYNE It was in your head, Knox. I knew you'd be the first to crack. You can't stick it any longer.

KNOX It was fierce, Butt. You must have heard it.

    GEORGE *up on the verandah is listening intently.*
    KEENEY *notices this.*

KEENEY Oh, the pranks and rascality we do be up to in the upper sixth dorm, George — you'd never guess. .

    GEORGE *goes into the office.*

KNOX (*To* BUTT) Maybe five or six screams. Then a kind of sobbing.

PYNE I'd watch that, Knoxie, if I was you.

KNOX You must have heard it, Butt. It was terrible.

PYNE It was the big blonde I had. I gave her her money but she kept yelling for an overtime bonus.

BUTT I heard it.

KNOX (*To* PYNE) There! There!

BUTT It was Smiler.

KNOX You see!

BUTT It was Smiler.

PYNE Jesus. Did they — ?

BUTT No. In his sleep.

> *Pause.*

PYNE It's almost every night now. Jesus, he must go through agonies.

KNOX I knew I heard it. I knew. I knew.

PYNE Jesus, the bastards — the bloody bastards.

> *A very brief silence. Then suddenly* KEENEY *leaps to his feet.*

KEENEY (*Very rapidly*) Good afternoon, children, and welcome to our dig. Your teacher tells me that none of you has ever seen an excavation before and you could well be excused for thinking that it does look more like a bomb-crater — or maybe a huge womb — or, as one of these men has suggested, like a prison yard with the high walls and the watch-tower up there and the naughty prisoners trying to tunnel their way out to freedom ha-ha-ha.

> PYNE *joins the game as the teacher — addressing a group of imaginary pupils around him.*

PYNE To freedom ha-ha-ha.

KEENEY Now as your teacher will have told you — Miss O'Driscoll, isn't it?

PYNE Flora O'Driscoll. But the children just call me Tits.

KEENEY As Miss O'D. will have told you, archaeology is the scientific study of people and their culture by analysis of their artefacts and inscriptions and monuments and other such remains.

PYNE I've told them a dozen times, Dr. King.

KEENEY And our excavations here extend from early Viking right down to late Georgian — in other words over a period of approximately a thousand years. So that what you have around you is encapsulated history, a tangible précis of the story of Irish man.

PYNE Repeat that — Irish man, Irish man.

Throughout KEENEY's *lecture,* PYNE *picks up the last two words of each sentence and repeats them sotto voce two or three times to impress them on 'her' pupils' minds. This echo does not interrupt the flow of 'King's' speech. And when the convention is established, 'Miss O'Driscoll' merely mouths the words.*

KEENEY To give you just one instance: from our diggings we have established what a man in the year 930, for example, had for his lunch, what clothes he wore, what games he liked, what musical instruments he played, what vegetables he planted in his garden. Isn't that marvellous?

PYNE Isn't that marvellous?

KEENEY And of course the more practical our information about our ancestors, the more accurate our deductions about his attitudes, the way he thought, what his philosophy was — in other words the more comprehensive our definition of him. And as I keep insisting to my helpers here (*confidential aside*) incidentally when we began this dig we had a full complement of ordinary labourers. But when our budget was exhausted we had to let them go and now we're reduced to — (*points with elaborate secrecy to the men scraping*) — and as the Swan of Avon says, they are not what they seem.

PYNE (*Repeating the gesture*) These?

KEENEY All volunteers.

PYNE How wonderful!

KEENEY Of a sort. And unpaid of course.

PYNE Why did they volunteer?

KEENEY A good question, Tits — why? Instinct?

PYNE Boredom?

KEENEY Disaffection?

PYNE Anger?

KEENEY Estrangement?

PYNE Necessity?

KEENEY Necessity?

PYNE I want five volunteers — you, you, you, you and you.

KEENEY Oh, that kind of necessity! No, they are all genuine volunteers.

PYNE Marvellous!

KEENEY But men, I'm afraid, of turbulent tendencies. But that's an intriguing story in itself.

PYNE Really?

KEENEY Tell you in bed tonight, Tits.

PYNE Oh, Doctor!

KEENEY (*Loudly again*) And as I keep insisting to my friends here, the more we learn about our ancestors, children, the more we discover about ourselves — isn't that so? So that what we are all engaged in here is really a thrilling voyage in *self*-discovery.

PYNE He makes it all so interesting.

KEENEY But the big question is: How many of us want to make *that* journey? Be that as it may, let's look around, shall we, and get a general picture first.

PYNE Into line, children. Butt, pay attention! Knox, leave yourself alone!

KEENEY Now, up here we have the remains of Georgian cellars. And below that is a bank of debris from Norman times.

PYNE Norman times — Norman times — Norman times.

KEENEY And beside us here . . . Excuse me, Knox, could you let the children through?

KNOX Fuck off.

KEENEY (*Aside*) Fluent Norse speaker; and although he does have the characteristic stature and odour of a Norseman, he is in fact much later. And almost certainly the last of the fertility symbols — wouldn't you agree?

PYNE Definitely.

KEENEY (*Loud again*) And here — here we have the remains of three centuries of waste. And where I stand — can you all see, children? — where this man (BUTT) is digging, we have the remains of a Viking house. Any exciting finds

37

today, Butt? (*Aside*) One of our most dedicated men. Married — adept with the trowel — ten kids. A real primitive but passionately interested.

PYNE How primitive?

KEENEY Startling. Tell you in bed tonight.

PYNE You rascal!

KEENEY (*Loud again*) Now this house, as you see, is a teeny-weeny place by our standards — it's really the size of a prison cell, isn't it? — but very compact and very cosy and I'm sure our Viking ancestor was idyllically happy in it. Known as a post-and-wattle house.

PYNE Post-and-wattle, post-and-wattle.

KEENEY Ash or elm uprights with hazel wattling. Clay floor. Fireplace in the centre. And around it at night sat our tenth century stonemason or farmer or sailor, combing and narding his tresses while his good wife, Mollusca, and her happy brood practised their swordsmanship.

PYNE Ab-sol-utely fascinating. And who is this gentleman?

KEENEY That, Miss O'D., is the genie of the land.

PYNE Is he . . . dead?

KEENEY Ah, there are two schools of thought about that. (*To* GEORGE, *who has returned to his table*) Wouldn't you agree, George?

GEORGE What about telling the kids the startling history of the diggers, Keeney?

PYNE Who is he, Professor?

KEENEY George — who accompanies me on all my excavations: site-manager, foreman, caretaker, and ass-licker of everyone in authority.

PYNE We work for an ass-licking gaff
Who considers his diggers riff-raff — Ha-ha.

DES (*Entering*) Am I the only one's frozen this morning? George!

GEORGE Hello.

DES In that brown parcel there's a new jar of coffee. Make us a cup, will you?

KEENEY (*Gripping* KNOX's *elbow*) My God, he's really hooked on it.

GEORGE Do you want it just now?

DES If you're not too busy.

GEORGE Actually I'm in the middle of —

DES Okay, okay, I'll make it myself.

GEORGE No, it's all right. I'll do it.

DES Thank you, George. Anyone else want a cup?

BUTT None for me.

PYNE Nor me.

DES Keeney?

KEENEY Damn it all — why not. A dash of San Francisco in the blood!

DES Knox?

Pause.

KEENEY The man's talking to you, Knoxie.

DES Do you want a cup of coffee?

KNOX Me? Christ, no; no, no, no, no, no. (KNOX *busies himself scraping*)

DES It's all right, Knox — I'm only asking you. What's wrong with that guy?

PYNE (*Going to pit*) Smiler might take a cup.

DES (*To* BUTT) Remember those seeds you found last June?

BUTT What seeds?

PYNE Smiler! Smiler Baby!

DES Remember — you got them inside a bowl in that lower Viking section.

BUTT Oh, those. Aye.

DES Well, they're . . . (*Produces a letter*) . . . Just got the report back from the lab . . .

PYNE Coffee!

DES (*Reads*) 'Chenopodium — goosefoot — pale persicaria.'

BUTT What's that?

DES 'Knot grass and black bindweed.'

BUTT Never heard of it.

DES Chenopodium is 'an edible weed with a green flower and includes the family of mangelwurzel and orach' — whatever they are.

KEENEY Quite common.

DES So apparently that was part of their diet.

KEENEY Anywhere the soil's alkaline.

DES Turn it off, Keeney, would you?

KEENEY Chenopodium — goosefoot — foot-loose — fancy-free — tickle-my-fancy — fancy-meeting-you-here — 'tell me where is fancy bred' — it has a lot of names. My grandmother used to boil it with nettles and give it to us.

DES That a fact?

KEENEY Yes. When we were young turkeys and she wanted to redden our combs.

He goes off with a bucket.

PYNE Ha-ha.

DES (*Calling*) Pity she didn't break your bloody neck!

Des goes towards the steps.

KNOX Hi, Butt, what's this?

KNOX *has unearthed a small piece of bone. The find is of routine interest; no excitement.*

BUTT Is it a bit of an antler?

KNOX I got it here.

BUTT It's bone. And there's some sort of a design.

PYNE Let's see.

KNOX Bugger off, you!

PYNE Sorry — sorry.

BUTT Probably a trial piece.

KNOX I knew it was a bone. It felt like a trial piece — you know — smooth.

BUTT It's an illustration of a ship. (*Increased interest*) Hi, Des, come here till you see this.

KNOX A ship — a ship — I just thought it was a ship.

PYNE I think it's a nuclear sub, Knoxie.

KNOX Is — ?

PYNE Ha-ha-ha.

KNOX Bugger you, Pyne!

BUTT (*To* DES) Look at the illustration.

DES Very clear, isn't it? A warship and one — two — three — four warriors. Who got it?

KNOX Me. I did. I got it.

DES Where?

KNOX Just there. At the corner.

DES Right, okay. I'll record it.

He moves towards the steps.

BUTT Des — is it a warship?

DES Didn't you see the four warriors?

BUTT She's very broad for a warship.

DES So?

BUTT That chart behind the office door — the one of all those ships in that Danish museum — it's the very same ship as the bottom one on that chart.

DES Are you sure?

BUTT I'm sure. And she's listed as a trader.

DES So she's a trader — an armed trader.

BUTT And on that chart she's dated 1150.

DES Okay. So she's a twelfth-century trader. Go to the top of the class.

BUTT But we found her here beside this house. And this house is tenth century. So the dating of that museum trader is . . . isn't right.

DES Come off it, Butt.

BUTT The chart's wrong, Des!

DES Don't be absurd.

BUTT Either the chart's wrong or the dating of this house is wrong.

DES Would it not occur to you that this (*trial piece*) mightn't belong to the same period as the house?

BUTT But it must — we're at boulder-clay level. The museum's wrong, Des.

DES Okay — okay — no need to get aggressive. We'll check it out calmly. All right — could we settle down now and get a bit of solid work done?

He goes up the steps.

KNOX Christ, what bit him?

BUTT The museum is wrong.

KNOX You're right, Butt. The moment I seen it I knew it was a trader.

KEENEY enters. His speech takes him right across the stage.

KEENEY Let us pray. Beloved Saint Persicaria, who in thy lifetime among the pagan eskimo didst vouchsafe to make the viola honoured and revered, we now beseech you to smile upon the endeavours of young Dolly Wilson who at this moment is doing her Grade Four Guildhall School of Music London practical. But only if success in her efforts would be in the interests of her immortal soul.

He goes off.

PYNE Amen. Ha-ha. Great aul' instrument, the viola, all the same. Ha-ha.

He goes off. Only BUTT and KNOX are left on the site-floor. Pause. KNOX moves closer to BUTT. His speech is a mixture of confidence and a reverie.

KNOX I learned the cello, Butt. Up till I was nine. Christ. (*Pause*) He used to come to the house every Thursday — an Italian fella. And at the end of the lesson my mother and the maid would bring us up tea and cakes on a big posh silver tray. And your man Vitelli — Christ, *that* was his name! How in Christ's name did I remember that? — he'd bow low and kiss my mother's hand and then he'd eat the cakes with his fingers out like this — eat every damned one of them down to the last crumb. And then my father would have the car sent round to drive him home to wherever it was he came from . . . Signor Vitelli . . . Christ, where did that name come out of . . . ?

He begins working again. BUTT, who stopped to listen to his story, still gazes at him for a few seconds. Then he, too, begins working. DES has been looking at the articles on the trestle-table, including the jug. He now goes into the office where GEORGE is making coffee. He consults the chart behind the door.

GEORGE We look at the pictures in a couple of professional journals and suddenly we're experts.

DES Mm?

GEORGE Next thing he'll be looking for a site of his own.

DES What are you talking about?

GEORGE Butt.

DES He might well be right.

GEORGE A thick customer, Butt.

DES Isn't that a good one — he could very well be right.

DES *leaves the chart and consults a book.*

GEORGE Your coffee.

DES In a minute.

GEORGE I finished the jug last night.

DES So.

GEORGE What do you think of it?

DES Pretty.

GEORGE Exquisite, isn't it?

DES Pretty.

Brief pause.

GEORGE Desmond, I'd appreciate it if you didn't order me about before the labourers.

DES Mm?

GEORGE I'm talking to you, Desmond.

DES What's that?

GEORGE The boss wants you to finish the photographing today.

DES Yes.

GEORGE He wants a complete series of the west section, especially the wall junction and the bank of debris.

DES Right.

GEORGE And all the sacks will have to be labelled and recorded before they're left up at the gate.

DES George, could I have time to check this first?

GEORGE As long as we get the whole place cleared up by this evening.

DES Are we expecting visitors?

GEORGE This is our last day.

DES What do you mean — our last day?

GEORGE I thought you knew. The dig's over.

DES The dig's over when the dig's finished.

KEENEY *enters and begins working.*

GEORGE I'm only repeating instructions, Desmond.

DES Whose instructions? What are you talking about?

GEORGE The boss called in yesterday after you left — all the stuff's being carted off on Monday and the builders move in on Tuesday.

DES What are you talking about, George?

GEORGE Dr. King's orders.

DES But we're not finished here! There's at least another two weeks work to be done! We haven't even touched that outer wall!

GEORGE Boss's orders!

DES Bloody marvellous! The speculators whistle once and Professor King says, 'It's all yours, boys. Sorry for holding you up' — a site the like of which this country has never seen before!

GEORGE The money's finished.

DES The money was finished three months ago. Money's not the problem. They're not paid. I'm not paid. For God's sake the royalties from his worthless books would keep this place going for six years. What do they say?

PYNE *enters and begins working.*

GEORGE They haven't been told yet.

DES I suppose they don't matter?

GEORGE I didn't say that.

DES So the only people in on the secret are you and King and the builders?

GEORGE And the museum board. And there's nothing secret about it. Wilson'll tell them over the weekend.

DES They'll be told now — by me.

GEORGE I don't think that's wise, Desmond.

DES Maybe not. But they did more work here than all of us put together. Is King at the museum?

GEORGE At a board meeting.

DES (*Preparing to leave*) Right. You just don't abandon a site like this because you've looted enough for another coffee-table book or because you've another fat site lined up for next year.

GEORGE Where are you going?

DES To the museum — to lodge a formal protest with the committee.

GEORGE Desmond, don't be hasty, don't do anything you'll —

DES *marches out of the office; stands on the verandah. He is angry but he is also conscious of the moment.*

DES I want you all to listen to me.

PYNE Quiet, there! Quiet! Quiet! Quiet!

DES I've something very important to tell you — something that affects all of us.

KEENEY A speech, be God, a speech!

PYNE Settle down there!

KEENEY Let the dog see the rabbit!

PYNE Silence!

KEENEY Quiet!

PYNE Quiet!

KEENEY Silence gentlemen, for Dessy the Red!

DES I've just learned from the site-manager that —

KEENEY I've been chosen Queen of the May!

PYNE Ha-ha.

DES — the dig ends this evening.

PYNE What's this? What's this?

DES Orders from Professor King.

PYNE The dig's over?

DES This is as big a shock for me as it is for you. And I'm going straight over to the museum now to see Dr. King and the board. And I'm going to tell them that if they allow the builders on to this site before our job is finished, I personally will write to every newspaper in the country and expose this act for what it is — a rape of irreplaceable materials, a destruction of knowledge that the Irish people have a right to inherit, and a capitulation to moneyed interests.

KEENEY That's good. That's impressive. God but I'm a sucker for that sort of stuff.

DES As for you men, no one knows better than myself how much toil and sweat you have put into this dig and I know that you are as angered by this news as I am. As to what form your anger will take, that is up to you. I appreciate that your circumstances are peculiar. But I also know that you are in the circumstances you are in because you are men of passionate conviction. And I just want you to know that whatever stance you take, whatever protest you think fit, it will be the right one and I will be fully and wholeheartedly behind you.

He runs down the steps and quickly off.
    BUTT *scarcely moves from his kneeling position.*
    KNOX *is not quite sure what has happened.*
    KEENEY *and* PYNE *stare after* DES *with exaggerated incredulity because they recognize that his speech and his exit were that bit too histrionic.*
    Pause.

PYNE By the Lord Harry.

KEENEY Well-well-well-well-well.

PYNE What was that all about?

KEENEY Good question. I think we've just been sacked.

PYNE Us? Never.

KEENEY Looks like.

PYNE (*Calls*) Hi, George, what's happening?

KEENEY In fact I'm sure of it.

PYNE Sacked?

KEENEY Booted.

PYNE Fired?

KEENEY Just like that.

PYNE God, that's heartbreaking. I mean to say, this is the first time in my life I've ever felt — you know what I mean like — fulfilled in my work.

KEENEY As the actress said to the bishop.

PYNE Ha-ha. Hi. Leif, you're redundant. Go up to the office

and George'll give you your cards.

KEENEY All the same it was a great speech.

PYNE Des's? Magnificent.

KEENEY Positively stirring.

PYNE No spittle nor nothing.

KEENEY That's a fact.

PYNE (*Holds face up for inspection*) Look. Dry as a bone. And I was right below him.

KEENEY The clichés were only cascading out of him. 'Whatever stance you take, whatever protest you think fit' — if he ever packs up this job he can walk straight into politics.

PYNE (*Sings*) 'Vote, vote, vote for Comrade Desmond.'

KEENEY He looks that part, too.

PYNE Hi, Keeney, he said something mighty funny.

KEENEY Everything he said was hilarious.

PYNE He said we were angry. Are we angry?

KEENEY Naturally we're furious.

PYNE That's okay. But you never told me your circumstances were peculiar.

KEENEY As for my convictions, by Christ they're so passionate you could grill lamb chops on them.

PYNE Ha-ha.

KNOX Is the job over, Butt?

KEENEY The perceptive Knox. Did you ever notice that about Knoxie? — Straight through the waffle and right to the kernel. Yes, Knoxie, back to the mailbags. But as Desmond says, boys, we ought to take up a stance.

PYNE Are yous mice or are yous men?

KEENEY What about a dignified withdrawal of labour?

PYNE Or a go-slow.

KEENEY Or lobby our T.D.

PYNE That's more like it.

KEENEY Did you ever lobby your T.D.?

PYNE Never.

KEENEY Or his wife?

PYNE Now you're talking. 'Deputy's wife lobbied by irate diggers'.

KEENEY 'But nothing uncovered,' says triumphant Mrs. Immaculata Kelly.

PYNE Ha-ha. (*He goes to cesspit*) Hi, Smiler!

KEENEY Have you any suggestions, Butt? We've got Desmond's word that he'll back us.

BUTT I'm going to finish this section.

KEENEY Did you hear that, Pyne?

PYNE What's that?

KEENEY I ask Buttie Boy here for his suggestions and d'you know what he says?

PYNE What?

KEENEY 'I'm going to finish this section.'

PYNE That's our Butt.

KEENEY Buttie's Aplomb and Other Stories. I didn't think they bred men like that any more.

PYNE Never underestimate Butt.

KEENEY I mean to say, he may be a poor peasant crofter but that's real public school — that's what that is. Don't be deceived by that rustic appearance. As good a man as Casabianca any day — that's what our Buttie is.

PYNE The boy stood on the burning deck
and he was playing cricket;
The captain bowled a spinning ball
and hit his middle wicket.
Ha-ha-ha.

KEENEY Or Francis Drake — Butt knows that story. D'you know it, Pyne?

PYNE What's that one?

KEENEY 'Sir Francis, Sir Francis, the Armada's within sight of the coast!' 'First I'll finish my game of bowls and then I'll thrash the Spaniards.'

PYNE Frightfully good.

KEENEY Marvellous aul' shite they taught you at school, too, Butt, wasn't it? And I'm sure you remember the one about Thomas More mounting the scaffolding. 'I pray you, Lord Lieutenant, see me safe up and for my coming down let me shift for myself.' D'you think did Leif say something like that when he was being hoisted?

PYNE Come on up, Smiler. We're sacked.

PYNE *goes off.*

KEENEY Marvellous bloody phoney lines. All the same when you were a kid and the Christian Brothers were beating the tar out of you, be Jaysus you'd have swopped your aul' crags for aplomb like that, wouldn't you, Buttie? Give us one of your crags and I'll give you a bite of a-plomb, eh? What am I talking about? You did, man. You have it.

Slowly and menacingly BUTT *gets to his feet, armed with a trowel.*

BUTT I'm going to close your mouth, Keeney.
PYNE (*Entering*) Hi, boys, where's Smiler? (*Crosses stage calling*) Smiler! Smiler!

He goes off.

BUTT I've stood your taunting day in and day out for the past five months and now I'm going to close your mouth for good.
KEENEY George, he's going to hit me, George!
PYNE (*Off*) Smiler!
BUTT Come on, Keeney, come on, come on! Give us some of your yap now, Keeney — give us some of your smart chat now. Just once more, Keeney, just once more!
PYNE (*Entering*) Smiler's gone, boys!
KEENEY Don't let him hit me, Pyne!
PYNE D'you hear me — Smiler's gone!

Very brief pause.

KEENEY Yes, we know — he's slipped out to the pub with Leif.
PYNE I'm not joking, Keeney. He's not here. (*The reaction is more than surprise — there is an element of panic*)
KEENEY He's in the pit.
PYNE He's not. He's not on the site.
KEENEY Are you sure?
PYNE Positive. I'm telling you — he's cleared.
KEENEY Christ almighty!

Very brief pause. Then KEENEY *rushes off, calling:*

Smiler! Smiler!

BUTT Did you look in the shed?

PYNE Not there.

BUTT (*Up to* GEORGE *who has appeared*) Is Smiler up there?

GEORGE No one up here.

KEENEY (*Off*) Smiler!

BUTT (*To* KNOX) Look out there. Quick! Quick!

KNOX Maybe he's —

BUTT Now!

> KNOX *shuffles off.* BUTT *runs up the steps.*

GEORGE You're not allowed into —

> BUTT *tosses him aside and goes into the office.*
> KEENEY *enters and as he runs across the stage he calls*:

KEENEY Smiler! Smiler!

> *He exits again.* BUTT *comes out of the office and goes behind it.*

BUTT Okay, Smiler, where are you? This is no time for fooling. Come on, Smiler, where are you?

> GEORGE *has come down the steps.*

GEORGE (*To* PYNE) When did you see him last?

KEENEY (*Off*) Smiler!

PYNE I don't know — a while ago — he was standing there, wasn't he? — Jesus, I don't know.

> BUTT *on verandah.* KEENEY *enters.*

BUTT He's not here.

KEENEY He's gone.

KNOX (*Enters*) No, he's not out there, Butt.

> *A long pause as they look at one another. Finally:*

GEORGE How long is he gone?

PYNE How would I know — half an hour — three-quarters — five minutes —

GEORGE Did he say anything to any of you?

PYNE Not to me he didn't. (*To* BUTT) Did he say anything to you?

BUTT No.

PYNE To you, Knoxie?

KNOX Nor me neither.

GEORGE Where would he head for?

BUTT D'you think he knows that himself?

GEORGE Where's he from?

PYNE Donegal.

GEORGE Would he head for there?

BUTT What for?

GEORGE Family — relations — friends.

BUTT You don't know what you're talking about.

GEORGE He must have some sort of a plan in his head.

PYNE Aul' Smiler? Jesus, sure he hardly knows his own name.

GEORGE *goes briskly towards the steps.* KEENEY *is standing at the bottom, blocking his way.*

GEORGE I've a phone-call to make. (*Pause*) Get out of the road. (*Pause*) I've got to notify the authorities that Smiler has escaped. Move, Keeney!

Pause.

BUTT He's right, Keeney. If it was anyone else but Smiler. Let him phone.

PYNE Butt's right.

BUTT It's for his own good, Keeney. With a man like Smiler it's not squealing.

GEORGE Move!

Pause.

PYNE (*Quickly*) We'll take a vote on it — George phones or he doesn't — which is it? — Butt?

BUTT Phones.

PYNE Knoxie?

KNOX I think he should phone.

PYNE So do I.

GEORGE Let me past, Keeney.

BUTT Let him past, Keeney.

PYNE You're only wasting time. The quicker he's found the better.

KEENEY Do me a favour, George, would you? Leave us alone for two minutes. I've something private to say to my friends here.

GEORGE I'm going to —

KEENEY What I have to say is of interest only to the criminal element. Just two minutes. Please. I'm asking a favour, George. Please.

GEORGE *looks around at the others.*

GEORGE Two minutes exactly. Then I'm phoning.

He goes off.

KEENEY (*Beaming*) My God, this is all very serious. Look at all those solemn faces.

BUTT What have you got to say, Keeney?

KEENEY Just a few words — nothing more than a few words — and I promise you, Pyne, there'll be no saliva.

BUTT Are you going to say what you have to say or not?

KEENEY Yes. Well. All I've got to tell you is this. That our fellow internees held a meeting the night before last — no, not really a meeting — a sort of kangaroo court. And they discussed again our defection in volunteering for this job. And they were unanimous that being sent to Coventry wasn't an adequate punishment for us. So the court ruled that a punishment to fit the crime of treason be meted. And the assembled brethren decided that the only fit punishment would be . . . capital.

PYNE Who told you this? When did you hear this?

KEENEY So there is to be a contrived riot in Block C probably next Monday night. And in the course of that riot they're going to take care of us — a fall from a roof — a tumble down a stairs — you know how accidents can happen in a chaotic situation —

KNOX Are they going to do us, Butt?

KEENEY Correct, Knox. They're going to do us — or at least some of us.

KNOX (*To* BUTT) Not the screws?

KEENEY Correct again, Knox.

PYNE Jesus, the man that comes near me will —

KEENEY Exactly. But what chance has Smiler? — None!

BUTT What chance has he out there?

KEENEY Very little, agreed, but still a chance. So the choice we have is to let him have that chance, however slender, or have him brought back to a certain accident. It's up to you, gentlemen; because if you all disagree with me, who am I to oppose the process of democracy? (*Calls*) Right, George, come and join us!

Pause. Then quick black-out.

ACT TWO

Late afternoon on the same day. Already a portion of the site has been cleared — e.g. the trestle-table and many of the plastic sacks are gone. BUTT *and* KNOX *enter and exit, carrying off timbers, buckets, etc.* GEORGE *is in the office, taking books from the shelves, charts off the walls, etc. We can hear* PYNE *off-stage singing a song.* KEENEY *is on the verandah, rinsing cups. He stops and listens to* PYNE'S *song. Then he joins with great gusto in the last line and as he sings it he joins* GEORGE *in the office. There he makes tea.* KEENEY *seems to have established a right to be in the office; and he is even more assured, more relaxed, than in Act One.* GEORGE *tries to ignore him.*

PYNE   (*Singing off*)
    Said the mother to the daughter fair,
    'Why did you stoop so low
    To marry a poor labouring boy
    around the world to go?
    Some noble lord might fancy you,
    great riches to enjoy . . .'

KEENEY   (*Joining in*) 'So why do you throw yourself away on a poor labouring boy?' (*Now in office*) Powerful aul' song that, too, isn't it, George? Boys, but there's nothing I like better than to hear men singing at their work. Gives you a wonderful aul' feeling of . . . reassurance, doesn't it? God's in his heavens and the eternal verities are still thumping along. Or maybe I'm being romantic, George, am I? What d'you think? (*Searches*) Milk — milk — (*finds it*) Ah. Of course I'm not talking about my own croaking. I mean to say I just threw in my couple of aul' bars there just to nettle you — as you well know. But I'll say that for old George: he's not easy riz, by God he's not. (*Reaching across* GEORGE) The professor wouldn't mind if I borrowed his Wedgwood mug, would he? No, he wouldn't. Aye, the very first day I slapped eyes on

54

you, you reminded me of the manager of the first bank I was posted to. At least once a week he'd say to me: 'Mister Keeney' — he was from Belmullet but the poor eejit thought that a Scotch accent was more appropriate for a bank manager — 'Mister Keeney, the client who always withdraws is no man.' And honest to God, George, I was an innocent cub in those days and I thought it was a class of dirty aul' chat he was at. D'you know does Buttie take sugar? Damnit it's good for him. (*Counts cups*) One — two — three — four — that's it. Pity we hadn't a wee cake now and the farewell party'd be complete. Aye, there used to be an aul' hoor in Derry. Spent her nights dodging about the quays. Her name was Vera McLaughlin but she was known as Eternal Verity — wasn't that apt? (*Searching*) A spoon — a spoon — (*discovers the jug*) Here — what's this? So this is where you have it?

GEORGE Don't you lay a —

KEENEY Smiler's pieces all put together and making a handsome jug! Oh you're a secretive wee man, too, George.

GEORGE Put that — !

KEENEY Well, isn't that elegant; very elegant indeed. Oh, the boys will have to see this, George. Oh, they've a right to see this. I mean to say, George, aesthetic delights aren't for the elite alone — as Dessy the Red'll tell you. But it's more than an aesthetic delight, this, George. This is an omen. What am I talking about — it's much more than an omen — it's a symbol, George. This is Smiler, George; Smiler restored; Smiler full, free and integrated. Or maybe I'm being romantic again, George, am I?

GEORGE Keeney, if you—

KEENEY Damnit no, I'm not. Not about Smiler. The rest of us now, we're different. I mean to say, we — well, not to put a tooth in it — we deliberately 'offended against the state', or to be strictly accurate, George, they interned us because of 'attitudes that might be inimical to public security'. But Smiler — d'you know Smiler's story? A stonemason from the west of Donegal; a quarry employing seven men; and Smiler's the shop-steward. And when they interned one of his mates, what d'you think the stupid bugger did but call his men out and set off on a protest march to Dublin! Can you imagine? Six thick quarrymen from the back of nowhere, led by Smiler, thumping across the country behind a tatty banner and a half-drunk mouth-organ. Well, of course they got about as far as the Derry border and there they whipped Smiler off to jail in Dublin and beat the tar out of him for twelve consecutive hours — you know, just as a warning. And begod it worked, George, worked like a spell. I mean to say, look at him now — a more civil man you couldn't meet in a day's travel. That's right — that's right. Course they give him the odd bleaching still — you know — just to keep him in trim. But it's kind of superfluous, wouldn't you say so? (*Admiring the jug*) All the same there's a victory there, George. Be Jaysus, George, I know he's going to defeat them.

GEORGE (*With quiet fury*) I'm giving you adequate warning now, Keeney, that when Mr. Wilson gets here I'm going to make a formal charge against you. One — that you connived at the escape of a fellow prisoner; and two — that you threatened violence against my person if I reported that escape to the appropriate authorities.

KEENEY (*Confused innocence*) Isn't that two charges, George?

GEORGE And I'll do all in my power to see that the full rigours of the law are applied against you.

KEENEY Believe me, George, even detectives in bad thrillers don't talk like that anymore. (*Lifts tray and exits*) Party-time! Party-time! (*Only* BUTT *is on stage as* KEENEY *descends. We can hear* PYNE *whistling off*) Call them in, Butt, for a farewell celebration. (*Calls*) Doctor Pyne, strawberries and cream on the lawn!

PYNE (*Off*) Coming!

> KEENEY *puts the tray down close to* BUTT *and speaks quietly, almost gently, but with a passion that is scarcely concealed.*

KEENEY I'm going to let you in on a secret, Buttie: I'm feeling reckless — no, not reckless — wild. You know on a Friday night after you've washed and shaved and put on the good suit and the pay-packet's in the pocket and the first half's sitting on the counter before you and you've an almost overwhelming sense of power and control and generosity and liberation — and yet at the same time there's nothing you'd like better than to smash something or go roaring down the street with a woman under each arm. Well, that's how I feel now, Butt — anarchic, is that the word? But sure who am I tellin'? Isn't that what has us all in bother?

BUTT I think we done the wrong thing, Keeney — you know, about Smiler.

KEENEY, *deliberately parodying his previous speech, now takes up a drunken, belligerent stance.*

KEENEY Come on, yous bastards, come on! Yous couldn't bate time with a toy drum!

BUTT We should have let George report him.

KEENEY Where's the father of Calvinism? (*Calls*) Knoxie!

BUTT We made a mistake, Keeney.

KEENEY A religious reformer called Knoxie
Made love to a Papist from Hoxie —

BUTT Any of the rest of us it would have been different.

KEENEY Cried she, 'Something's wrong!
There's a terrible pong!
It's the smell of your unorthodoxy!'

BUTT Smiler's special. You know that yourself.

KEENEY You agreed that he take his chance.

BUTT Only because that's the way you were all voting.

KEENEY He may make it. You never know.

BUTT Make it! How can Smiler make it!

KEENEY He thinks he can.

BUTT He doesn't know the day of the week it is. And when they catch him, they really will kill him this time — you know that.

KEENEY Yes, they'll kill him. Or his own mates'll kill him — or kill you or me or Pyne or Knox. Yes, one way or the other there's going to be a bloodletting. But at least now he's not going to be a volunteer. And then again, Buttie Boy, you never know, he might escape — remember, fools have a long and impressive history of immunity.

PYNE *enters*.

PYNE Great! Where did the tea come from?

KEENEY The provident George — who else?

PYNE One decent man. (*Calls up*) God's blessing on you and yours, George. You wouldn't have an aul' loaf of bread or an aul' pair of shoes or an aul' jacket you don't need? Ha-ha.

BUTT I was just saying to Keeney that —

PYNE Which (*cup*) is mine?

KEENEY Any one at all.

PYNE If I drank out of the boss's mug, d'you think it would make me smart? (*To* KNOX *who has just entered*) Here you are, boy.

KNOX It isn't that coffee, is it?

PYNE You're a suspicious bastard, too, Knoxie. It's tea, man. D'you want it or do you not?

KNOX Ta.

BUTT I was saying to Keeney I think we should get George to phone in and say that —

KEENEY *produces the jug with a flourish.*

KEENEY Gentlemen, the item you've been waiting for!

PYNE What's that?

GEORGE *has discovered that the jug is missing. He comes out on to the verandah.*

KEENEY Lot 142 — the unique Burgundy Jug discovered in Ireland in the 1970s by Professor Smiler!

BUTT Is it . . . ?

PYNE It's the lad, by God!

KEENEY Nothing less. And what can I say to connoisseurs like yourselves except that the only other comparable piece is one of the most treasured possessions of the British Museum and that in my long career in the art world never before have I had the privilege of handling an item

58

of this distinction. Gentlemen, what am I offered for Smiler's Jug?

PYNE Ha-ha. (*Calls*) Hi, George, you might pick up a bargain here!

GEORGE *comes slowly down the steps.*

BUTT Show me.

KEENEY Certainly.

KNOX (*Privately to* PYNE) What's he drinking his tea out of that for?

PYNE Jesus, Knox, you can take you nowhere.

KEENEY 'To what green altar, O mysterious priest,
Lead'st thou that heifer lowing at the skies.'
Well, Buttie?

BUTT He made a great job of it.

KEENEY Didn't he?

BUTT Good.

KEENEY Beautiful, isn't it?

BUTT It's good.

KEENEY (*Quietly*) I knew you'd like it.

PYNE Show me it. (KEENEY *gives the jug to* PYNE)

KEENEY Right, gentlemen, make me a bid. What am I offered? Everything must be disposed of today.

GEORGE (*Now beside* PYNE) I'll take that.

GEORGE *and* KEENEY *both reach for the jug.* KEENEY *gets it.*

KEENEY Now, now, now, George, don't be a spoilsport.

GEORGE Give it to me.

KEENEY If you have an offer to make, George, put up your hand like everybody else.

GEORGE *is now between* PYNE *and* KEENEY *who pretend they are going to throw it over and back across his head.*

PYNE (*Clapping his hands*) Here, Keeney, here, here!

GEORGE Give it to me, Keeney.

KEENEY Sing us a song, George, and I'll give it to you.

GEORGE Hand it over.

KEENEY (*Sings*) 'She was only the sergeant's daughter . . .'

PYNE Over his head, Keeney! Over his head!

KEENEY 'But she let the county inspect-or'

GEORGE I'm asking you, Keeney.

PYNE Quick, man, quick!

GEORGE I've warned you already!

KEENEY (*To* BUTT) Maybe this is what I should smash — what d'you think?

PYNE Throw — throw — throw!

GEORGE (*Turning to* BUTT) All right — I'm holding you responsible for that jug. Anything happens to that jug, Butt, it's your responsibility. Remember that.

GEORGE *goes off.*

PYNE (*Calling after him*) Don't you worry, George. I'll keep an eye on it. Ha-ha.

BUTT (*To* KEENEY) Come on. Cut out the fooling. I don't want any accidents with that. Leave it up where it belongs.

KEENEY Now that's a curious phrase — 'where it belongs'. Where does it belong? Is it Smiler's — finders keepers? Or is it the Professor's? Or does it belong to the nation? Or does it belong to — Brother Leif. Damnit, that's a thought! And if it's Leif's, isn't it about time he got it back?

PYNE Bloody good idea!

KEENEY *places the jug at Leif's feet.*

KEENEY And when you think of it, what safer place could it be than in the vaults of a 150-storey hotel?

PYNE Look! He's smiling. He says thanks very much — he was lost without it.

KEENEY Isn't that nice? The courtesy of the older generation. (*He crouches beside Leif and keeps looking at him throughout the following sequence*) All the same that's a fair big hole in the top of the skull. A clout like that would knock the thought of women out of your head for

60

a couple of hours, wouldn't it?

PYNE Speak for yourself. I damn-near died of a fractured skull in New York. Going back on board and slipped on the bloody gangway. Fourteen weeks I was on my back, but I swear to God — I'm not joking — it was thinking about women all the time that pulled me through.

KEENEY (*Quietly, still staring at Leif*) Talk to me about him, Butt.

PYNE The doctors said it was a bloody miracle.

KEENEY What sort of man was he, Butt?

PYNE Leif? I'll tell you everything about him. What d'you want to know?

KEENEY Was he a Friday-night man? Did he think he was invincible? Did he challenge them all? Or was he a husk, like George, a cliché? Tell me about him, Butt.

PYNE I'll tell you. I read the whole inside story in the Sunday papers.

KEENEY *suddenly leaps to his feet.*

KEENEY (*With excessive enthusiasm*) Right, Pyne! You tell us! We'll start with you! You tell us his story!

PYNE Well, children . . .

KEENEY We're off!

PYNE Once upon a time . . .

KEENEY Tits O'Driscoll!

PYNE Behave yourself, Keeney.

KEENEY Yes, Miss, sorry, Miss.

PYNE Once upon a time . . .

KEENEY 'Once upon a time' — ah sure thanks be to God, lads, it's only an aul' yarn.

PYNE Once upon a time there were two cousins. One was tall and fair and his name was Ulf; and the other was small and ginger and his name was Leif.

KEENEY 'The one red leaf, the last of its clan.'

PYNE Jesus, d'you want to hear the story or do you not?

KEENEY We're all ears — aren't we, Butt? (*To* PYNE) Go ahead — 'and his name was Leif'.

PYNE And they lived in a modest little settlement at the top of a fjord.

KEENEY Now wasn't that grand entirely.

PYNE And when they were still little boys their families decided to emigrate from Norway and they sailed for Ireland and settled in a colony here and became Christians.

KEENEY Settled where?

PYNE On this very spot.

KEENEY Where we stand?

PYNE Just there.

KEENEY (*With reverence*) The holy ground. (*Suddenly sings*) 'Once more, boys —'

KEENEY
PYNE } (*Together*) '— once more — the holy ground once more.'

They break off. PYNE *laughs.*

PYNE Now I'm bloody lost. Where was I?

KEENEY Little Ulf and little Leif — Ulfeen and Leifeen — gulpin and elfin —

KNOX Why don't you shut up, Keeney!

KEENEY *turns to him in amused astonishment.*

KEENEY Now there's a compliment for you, Pyne.

PYNE Thank you, Knox.

KEENEY Relax, Knoxie. Your turn's coming. (*Confidentially to* BUTT) Over-eager — that's his problem.

PYNE And as they grew up the the two little boys were inseparable. Everything Ulf did, Leif did the same. And when they were both sixteen they signed on the same tanker and sailed together to Greenland and North Africa and the Middle East and up the Baltic . . .

KEENEY 'Once upon a time' — keep up the protection of the myth.

PYNE And then in their twenty-first year they were both crewmen on the first Viking ship to discover America.

KEENEY Hurrah!

PYNE And they never had a time together like the time they had there — between hunting and fighting and Indian women and making expeditions inland together. Leif wanted to settle down there but after a few months Ulf became homesick; and even though it was the month of February, nothing would satisfy him but they'd equip a ship and set out for home.

KEENEY For Norway.

PYNE Here — this was their home now.

KEENEY Of course. Merely trying to divert them.

PYNE So Ulf loaded the ship with all the booty he could lay hands on; and Leif — all he took with him was the Indian girl he'd set up with out there. And on their way back they were torn to pieces by the winter gales, and Ulf and his booty were washed overboard, and the only two to make it back were Leif and his woman.

KEENEY (*To* BUTT) Ah, shure I can schmell dishaster comin'.

PYNE And instead of welcoming them, the two families stared at Leif and his brown woman and said, 'Where's Ulf? And who is this black pagan?' And although Leif told them about the terrible Atlantic gales, they said, 'No. This black woman is evil. She killed our Ulf. Now you and she must die.'

KEENEY Don't you know!

PYNE And they burned the Indian woman before Leif's eyes. And then they put a rope round his neck, and strung him up, and just for good measure opened his skull. And there he is. Brother Leif. Jesus, I didn't know how that was going to end!

Just as PYNE *finishes* GEORGE *enters. He is taking site photographs.*

KEENEY (*Clapping*) Not bad, Pyne. Fairly trite melody but an interesting sub-theme. Not bad at all.

PYNE Not bad? It was bloody good. Out of the top of my head, too! Wasn't it bloody good, Knoxie?

KEENEY (*Very rapidly*) Why did he come back?

PYNE Who?

KEENEY Leif.

PYNE He had to come back.

KEENEY Why?

PYNE Sure he had to come back with his mate, hadn't he?

KEENEY Why?

PYNE   Jesus, Ulf was his mate, wasn't he?

KEENEY   Is that why he came back?

PYNE   (*Blustering, confused*) Why the hell do you think he came back! He wasn't going to stay out there by himself, was he? 'Why did he come back?' — Such a stupid bloody question. 'Why did he come back?' — Jesus, that's the stupidest question I ever heard!

GEORGE   Stand where you are, Pyne. You, too, Keeney.

PYNE   (*Irritably*) What for?

GEORGE   To give the picture a scale. Go on talking.

PYNE   (*To* KEENEY) Oh, Lord, I'm sure I'm a sight! And these old flat shoes, too! Oh heavens!

> KEENEY *flashes on a brilliant smile and becomes an American matron while* GEORGE — *the reporter* — *takes pictures.*

KEENEY   Let me tell you: just before we left Baton Rouge, Louisiana, the travel agent warned Ethel and I that we might experience some civil commotion in your country. But I can tell you right now, sir, that we had a simply wunnerful time and we want your Irish readers to know that, too.

PYNE   Just fan-tastic.

KEENEY   As soon as we landed at Shannon we were frisked by two of your enormous guards — remember, Ethel?

PYNE   Oh my! And were they thorough!

KEENEY   And when we got to Dublin we were frisked again.

PYNE   Five minutes each!

KEENEY   Everywhere we went it was the same — hotels, bars, cinemas. Sometimes they were regular cops but more often they were plainclothes men.

PYNE   We were frisked right round the Ring of Kerry.

KEENEY   And all over Connemara.

PYNE   Tell him about the Aran Islands, Katie.

KEENEY   Yeah — special branch men — they told us themselves. In wellingtons and cloth caps. It was just frisk, frisk, frisk day and night for almost a week.

PYNE   Truly wunnerful.

KEENEY   And we just want your readers to know how grateful we are.

PYNE Ha-ha.

GEORGE All that stuff's got to be shifted up to the gate — when you're finished your tea-break.

He goes briskly off.

PYNE Hi, George, will you send us copies of the photos? Fame and fortune at last, Buttie.

Enter DES. He looks very solemn.

Look at who's here! Yes, Dessy boy. Well, how did it go?

DES Hi.

He goes straight up the steps.

PYNE Did you lay into them, give them the old one-two-three, tell them to stick their bloody job — ?

PYNE breaks off because KEENEY, without taking his eyes off DES, puts a restraining hand on PYNE's arm.
They all watch DES go straight into the office where he picks up his shoulder-bag and two books. He comes down the steps again.

PYNE We're having a bit of a party. What'll it be — Scotch or Irish?

DES stops beside the group. After a brief pause he speaks, choosing his words very carefully.

DES Actually the board meeting was over when I arrived. But the boss was there and I said what I had to say to him. He wants you to know that he understands your . . . frustration. But as he pointed out the building contractors have already given us three extensions. And as a matter of fact — and this is something I wasn't aware of — only for their subsidy we'd have had to close long ago. But apart

65

from that altogether, digging is only part of the work, and the assessing of the stuff we actually have in hand is going to occupy all our time for the next eight months — right up to our next dig. In fact the boss wants me to start on that right now. So all in all . . . Good luck, Knox: you were a big help.

KNOX Luck.

DES Good luck, Butt.

BUTT I've a journal of yours.

DES Doesn't matter. Hold on to it. And if you feel like keeping up your interest in the game, just get in touch with me. Pyne — see you. Keeney. Where's Smiler?

BUTT He's —

PYNE He's in the bog.

DES Say goodbye to him for me.

PYNE Sure.

DES That's everybody. I'll be seeing George over the weekend. Okay? Thanks. We had a good time.

He moves off uncertainly. After he has gone a short distance KEENEY *speaks with pretended embarrassment.*

KEENEY The trouble is, Desmond, that you've put us in a sort of an awkward spot now. (DES *stops and turns*) You see, when you said you'd be behind us in whatever stance we'd take, naturally we thought you meant . . . (*To others*) It's not a secret, is it?

PYNE He'll find out anyway, won't he?

DES *watches* KEENEY *very closely, trying to determine if he's serious or joking.*

KEENEY Well, after you left we had a meeting, Desmond — you know — the lads here —

PYNE Be fair to George — George didn't take part.

KEENEY That's true — George wasn't involved . . . Anyhow we considered various suggestions — you know — how best to register our objections to the rape of the site and the destruction of knowledge that the Irish people have a right to inherit and be sustained and enriched by — all that sort of stuff — you know. And after one hell of a lot of to-ing and fro-ing and quite frankly one hell of a lot of soul-searching — (*To* PYNE) Didn't we search our souls?

PYNE With fine-combs and flash-lamps.

KEENEY The decision we came to, Desmond, was that the most effective protest we could make would be the one you yourself suggested and —

DES The one I . . . ?

KEENEY We wrote a letter to the papers.

PYNE (*Searching pockets*) I've a copy here somewhere —

KEENEY But you can rest assured, Desmond, we've said nothing in that letter that you yourself haven't said repeatedly over the past months. Right?

PYNE Absolutely. When you read it you'll be proud of it.

KEENEY Damnit, I've forgotten — we surely didn't leave out Desmond's name from the signatures, did we?

PYNE Afraid so.

KEENEY Hell!

PYNE But we quoted him in the last paragraph.

KEENEY That itself.

DES Is this one of their peculiar jokes, Butt?

BUTT *deliberately turns away from him and goes to the far end of the stage where he busies himself with sacks.*

KEENEY Dear Sir: We, the undersigned — a fairly crude para-phrase but the sentiments are accurate — we think the Irish people should know that the enormously valuable archaeological treasure-house — that was Pyne's phrase . . .

PYNE (*Beaming*) Good?

KEENEY . . . it is being shut down because Professor King has been bribed by the speculators to say that the dig is finished, even though it isn't, and because he has looted enough material to make another of his Auntie Coco coffee-table books —

PYNE Knoxie's phrase. Right, Knoxie?

KEENEY Then words to the effect that although the readers might consider *us* less than reliable, the anxiety we felt was shared by an honest and fair-minded young scholar who had toiled unselfishly here with us — by name Dessy the Red.

PYNE He's taking a hand at you — we didn't put in 'the Red' bit.

KEENEY Was there anything else?

PYNE The line about the sit-in.

KEENEY Oh, yes. We said there'd be a series of sit-in protests on the site every day at noon, beginning next Monday; and that strawberries and cream would be provided by George, learned talks by Butt, and authentic atmospheric smells by Knoxie. And then we all put our names at the bottom.

PYNE And Leif's.

KEENEY And Ulf's.

PYNE And Wilson's.

KEENEY And young Dolly's.

PYNE And George's.

KEENEY And de Valera's.

PYNE And Master McGrath's.

KEENEY And King Kong's.

PYNE And Hitler's.

KEENEY And me great uncle Billy McCluskey who had a hare-lip and went down with the *Titanic*.

PYNE A smashing letter, Des. Full of exclamation marks and things.

KEENEY He'll see it himself tomorrow. Any tea left?

Brief pause as DES *controls his anger and searches for calm words.*

DES Over the past five months, Keeney, I thought I had come to understand you people and maybe even to have a measure of sympathy with you. But by God I think now that hanging's too good for you.

As he marches off PYNE *blows a kiss after him and calls.*

PYNE A student called Dessy the Red —

KEENEY Preferred fellow subversives all dead.
I may quote Karl Marx,
But it's really for larks.
He's much better not done, only said.

PYNE Ha-ha.

KEENEY Indeed — indeed — indeed. Did you ever write to the papers, Knoxie?

PYNE Knoxie? Every week. Dear Auntie May, the girls all shun me. I suffer from smelly feet. What do you advise?

KEENEY Lag your feet and legs with asbestos soaked in rum for three weeks. And if that doesn't work, try washing them. (*To* GEORGE *who has just entered*) You've just missed Desmond, George. He really gave it to King. And for his honesty he's been kicked out of the faculty. Do you call that fair, George?

GEORGE *ignores him; goes straight up to his office.*

PYNE But he's unrepentant.

KEENEY Beaten but unbowed and sustained by a cast-iron certainty — like Brother Butt here. Isn't he lucky? And he says to tell you he enjoyed working with you . . .

PYNE Oh, he fancies George.

KEENEY . . . even though you're a sycophantic aul' bollicks and hanging would be too good for you. (*To* PYNE) I'm not misquoting him, am I?

PYNE His very words.

KEENEY (*To* KNOX *who is about to exit with a barrow*) Where are you off to, Knoxie? Hold on, man, you were about to tell us Leif's story, weren't you?

PYNE So he was. Good old Knoxie — your turn.

KEENEY Quiet, gentlemen, please.

PYNE Don't be shy, man. Face the company.

KEENEY The Knox version, friends.

KNOX *stands facing upstage.*

PYNE Come on, Knoxie. Once upon a time.

KEENEY Once upon a time there was a raggedy old man called Leif who scraped together a living by painting an odd boat or by running messages for sailors or by getting them back on board when they were drunk. But what nobody knew was that Leif was the only child of a merchant prince and that tutors from all over Europe came to his house to educate his precious son.

PYNE Oo-la-la! Very posh!

KEENEY But one day when the merchant prince was out riding a boar ran across his path — daddy's horse reared — daddy was thrown — daddy's neck was broken . . .

PYNE Click!

KEENEY . . . and of course daddy's empire collapsed with daddy because mammy was an idiot and all young Leif could do was say 'I own a well-trained falcon' in seven languages.

PYNE And play the viola.

KEENEY Of course. Which he played first in the taverns and then in the streets. But many's the night young Leif crept into his viola and slept in doorways and cried with hunger and loneliness. And then he made a major discovery.

PYNE What was that?

KEENEY He discovered that certain people — let's not be diffident — subversives — they were willing to pay him for carrying messages from one clandestine group to another — pay him not only with money and food and lodgings but with their companionship. And that discovery was more important to Leif than his music or his logic or his astrology or his rhetoric or his —

KNOX, *still facing upstage, bursts into tears of anger and embarrassment.*

KNOX Fuck you, Keeney! Fuck you! Fuck you! Fuck you!

KNOX *rushes off.*

KEENEY He's not upset, is he?

PYNE Ah come on, Knoxie. It's only a bit of fun, man. (*To others*) Jesus, poor aul' Knoxie. (*Runs off after* KNOX) Come on back and finish your tea, man. (KEENEY *looks after* PYNE. *The exhilaration — the 'wildness' — has died in him*)

KEENEY (*Wearily*)
There once was a nanny named Pyne
Who was blessed with a nature divine . . .

> *A weary laugh — he loses interest in his rhyme. Turns and looks at* BUTT. *Pause.*

And then suddenly, Butt, for no apparent reason the Friday-night man goes limp. All the wildness and power evaporate and all that's left is a mouth. Of course there is a reason — my overriding limitation — the inability to sustain a passion, even a frivolous passion. Unlike you, Butt. But then your passions are pure — no, not necessarily pure — consistent — the admirable virtue, consistency — a consistent passion fuelled by a confident intellect. Whereas my paltry flirtations are just . . . fireworks, fireworks that are sparked occasionally by an antic imagination. And yet here we are, spancelled goats complementing each other, suffering the same consequences. Is it ironic? Is it even amusing?

> BUTT *moves closer to* KEENEY. *The exterior is calm but the eyes are burning.*

BUTT I can tell you his story.

KEENEY Yes.

BUTT I know his story.

KEENEY I'm sure you do. That Gaelic head.

BUTT Yes, I know it. But you're wrong — not here (*tapping his head*) but here in my guts. Yes, I can tell you his story.

KEENEY (*Suddenly alert again*) I know your version, Butt. A poor Viking slave who rowed his masters across the seas on their plundering expeditions; until one morning suddenly all the muscles of his body atrophied with exhaustion and then because he could never row again they disposed of him.

BUTT Yes.

KEENEY Or he was a blacksmith who tramped the country shoeing other men's horses and then one day he asked: 'Why can't I have a horse of my own?'

BUTT Yes, Keeney.

KEENEY Or he was a carpenter who had built a whole Viking village and then asked to be allowed to keep one house for himself.

BUTT Yes, Keeney.

KEENEY Or he was a crofter who sucked a living from a few acres of soggy hill-farm — a married man with a large family. And then one day a new landlord took over the whole valley and he was evicted because he had no title.

BUTT Yes, Keeney, yes.

KEENEY Maybe yes. But for Christ's sake not with the assurance of your yes!

BUTT Or he was a bank-clerk who had courage and who had brains and who was one of the best men in the movement.

KEENEY Once upon a time.

BUTT Yes, Keeney. And you're sure of it in your guts, too.

KEENEY I'm sure of nothing now.

BUTT You were once. You shouted yes louder than any of us.

KEENEY Did I?

BUTT Five — six months ago. Before you volunteered for this job. You knew where you stood then. Are you going soft, Keeney?

PYNE and KNOX enter. Between them is SMILER. They have him by the arms.

PYNE Ta-ra-ra! Look who's here!

BUTT Good God!

PYNE What about this for a surprise?

BUTT Bloody Smiler!

PYNE Walks in the gate as cool as you like.

KNOX 'Where's Butt?' — That's all he says — 'Where's Butt?'

BUTT Bloody bastard! I thought he'd deserted us. Look at him, will you — the bloody bastard!

BUTT goes quickly to SMILER and embraces him with undisguised affection and relief.

KNOX There you are. Safe as houses.

PYNE And the cap as jaunty as ever. (*Calls*) Hi, George, look who's here!

KNOX 'Where's Butt?' — That's all he says.

BUTT Where did you find him?

GEORGE *is watching from the verandah.*

PYNE I'm telling you — just walked in the gate.

BUTT Where had he been? Where had he gone?

PYNE Who cares? He's back, isn't he? D'you see, George?

KNOX 'Where's Butt? Where's Butt?' He-he-he.

PYNE (*Boxing*) Okay, Smiler Baby. Put them up.

BUTT Smiler, you bastard, I was worried sick about you.

PYNE Weren't we all?

BUTT Where did you go to, man? Where have you been?

Pause. Finally:

SMILER That's right, Butt — that's right.

BUTT, KNOX *and* PYNE *explode with laughter as if* SMILER *had said something brilliantly witty. Throughout this whole sequence — from* SMILER'S *entrance until* KEENEY *speaks further down —* KEENEY *is standing by himself, rigid, tense, barely able to control himself.*

PYNE (*Laughing*) That's right — he says! That's right!

BUTT (*Laughing*) Oh my God, Smiler — you bastard!

PYNE That's right.

BUTT Sit down, sit down, sit down, man. Get him tea. Get him hot tea.

All three lead SMILER *downstage and sit him down. In their fussing over him they bump into one another.*

PYNE He can take mine.

BUTT Is it warm enough?

KNOX Mine's warm.

PYNE Show me. (*Feels the cup*) Yes, that's warmer.

BUTT Give me. (*He puts the cup into* SMILER'S *hands and holds it there*) His hands are cold. He's all cold.

PYNE Get him a coat.

BUTT Anyone got a coat?

PYNE I've none.

KNOX Neither have I.

BUTT Give me that sack.

KNOX Is it dry?

PYNE It's fine.

BUTT Give me.

He drapes a very large sack round SMILER'S *shoulders. It is so long that it hangs down his sides and looks like a ritualistic robe, an ecclesiastical cope.*

SMILER I walked along the street and —

BUTT You're okay, Smiler. You're okay now. Don't talk, man. You're fine now.

PYNE What about his feet? Those damn wellingtons aren't comfortable.

BUTT (*As he takes off the wellingtons*) Where are his boots?

PYNE They're over there, Knoxie. Get them.

BUTT Drink your tea, Smiler. Drink it up, man.

KNOX (*With the boots*) Here.

PYNE His feet are frozen.

BUTT Rub them with your hands.

PYNE (*As he massages one foot*) You do that one, Knoxie.

BUTT He must have sat somewhere for a long time.

PYNE How are the hands?

BUTT Warming up a bit. We'll soon have him perfect, won't we, Smiler?

KNOX (*Offering packet*) Would you like a fag, Smiler?

PYNE Jesus, Smiler, it must be Christmas!

BUTT Smiler doesn't smoke.

PYNE He'll smoke one of Knoxie's! He'll never get a chance again! Right, Smiler?

PYNE *puts a cigarette into* SMILER'S *mouth.* KNOX *lights it.*

KNOX Good fags, Smiler. Dear ones.

BUTT (*Holding the hands still*) They're warming up.

PYNE Okay, boy?

BUTT He's okay. He's back again. He's okay now.

PYNE The colour's coming back to his cheeks, too. Good old Smiler. (*Turns to* KEENEY) Looking great, isn't he?

KEENEY (*After a brief pause*) He's an imbecile! He's a stupid, pig-headed imbecile! He was an imbecile the moment he walked out of his quarry! And that's why he came back here — because he's an imbecile like the rest of us! Go ahead — flutter about him — fatten him up — imbecile acolytes fluttering about a pig-headed imbecile victim. For Christ's sake is there no end to it?

> KEENEY *goes off. The suddenness and passion of his outburst have stunned the others. They look at one another in shock. Pause.*

PYNE (*Attempting brightness*) What in the name of Jesus was that . . . was that all about? (*The words die. Brief silence. He attempts another rally — this time shadowboxing with* SMILER) Okay, Smiler Baby, put them up, man, put them up — boom-boom-boom — one-two-three — he's cold out — bang-bang-bang — right on the chin . . . (*Again the words wither. He looks at the others with a mixture of panic and anger*) Imbecile! He's the only imbecile here, for Jesus sake! Am I right, Butt? If anyone's a bloody imbecile, it's bloody Keeney — amn't I right, Butt?

BUTT It's just that he's afraid.

PYNE (*Aggressively*) Who's afraid? I'm not afraid!

BUTT Keeney.

KNOX What's he afraid of, Butt?

BUTT He's the one persuaded us to volunteer for this job — that's one of the reasons they hate him. He's the one they'll go for first — that's one of the reasons he's afraid.

KNOX Now that the job's over, Butt, there'll be no trouble? Now that we're back with them there'll be no trouble.

PYNE (*To* BUTT) Are you afraid?

BUTT I'm . . . I'm not sure any more.

GEORGE *comes bustling down the steps. Now that* SMILER *is back everything is well.*

GEORGE (*Being pleasant*) Come on, men, come on — Mr. Wilson'll be here any minute; and we don't want him to find us sitting down on the job and us in the last lap, do we? Are we going to get the site cleared or are we not? You wouldn't want to leave the place in a mess like this.

PYNE Bloody housewife, George.

GEORGE Take all the sacks out of the shed and leave them lying beside the gate. There's a couple lying back there.

PYNE All right, all right, all right.

He goes off.

GEORGE Knoxie, wash out all the wheelbarrows with the hose and then leave them lying upside down. (KNOX *goes*) You give him a hand, Smiler.

BUTT Smiler sits where he is — he's still cold.

GEORGE Is he? Oh in that case certainly — certainly. Would you like to sit up at the fire for a while, Smiler?

BUTT Leave him where he is.

GEORGE Whatever you say. You look after the planks, will you? And if you come across any trowels or brushes, give them to me.

GEORGE *goes off.* BUTT *begins picking up the timbers that are littered all over the floor.*

SMILER Yes, Butt.

BUTT Yes, Smiler.

SMILER Butt, I . . .

SMILER *gets to his feet. He is staring straight ahead and his mouth is working as if he were trying to capture some elusive intelligence.* BUTT *goes to him.*

BUTT What is it, Smiler?

SMILER When I went up to the gate, I wanted to run away — I knew I had to run away — I knew that — I knew that —

I — I —

BUTT Easy, man, easy.

SMILER And then when I was outside, I — I — I — I didn't know anymore — I didn't know anything, Butt — and I had to come back — to come — to —

BUTT Shhh.

KEENEY — to come back to you 'cos you'd tell me what to do — what to — what — what —

BUTT Easy — easy — easy.

SMILER Was that right, Butt? Was that right?

BUTT We'll see, Smiler. We'll see. We'll see.

SMILER We'll see?

BUTT Yes, we'll see, Smiler. We'll see. (*Whatever it was* SMILER *was about to capture has escaped him. His face softens into its usual witless smile*) Okay now, Smiler?

SMILER That's right.

BUTT That's right. Why don't you go and change out of those? You'll be more comfortable in your own clothes.

As SMILER *exits* KNOX *enters quickly, furtively. He is carrying something under his jacket. He looks about to make sure* BUTT *is alone.*

KNOX Psst — psst — psst, Butt. Come here — come here — come here.

BUTT What?

KNOX Come here till you see this.

BUTT *joins him downstage.*

Look, man, look.

He produces a paper bag and opens it.

BUTT What is it?

KNOX Look at that.

BUTT I can't see.

KNOX Some of the things I found myself. Some of them I swiped out of the office.

BUTT What have you got?

KNOX Pieces of brooches, bones, bits of combs, trial pieces, scraps of leather, broken rings —

BUTT What do you want them for?

KNOX What d'you think! Christ, they're worth a fortune!

BUTT Knoxie —

KNOX Antiques, man! There's a small fortune there, man!

BUTT Knoxie, they've no —

KNOX Shh. Too much for me to smuggle out by myself. But if you take half of them, we'll make a deal — I'll go fifty-fifty with you. We'll be made for life, Butt.

BUTT I'm telling you — they're not worth —

KNOX I'll put your share into your boots and tonight we'll —

He breaks off because GEORGE *enters. He shuffles off.*

GEORGE I can tell you, Butt, I'm as relieved as you are that Smiler came back to us. I mean, you fellows did a good job here and it would have given me no pleasure to report you. For as I've said to Mr. Wilson, you helped us out of a fix and I would hope that this experience has given you something — you know, new interests, new insights. (*Lowers his voice*) Butt, it's none of my business and you can tell me to shut up if you like; but I'm going to give you a bit of advice.

BUTT What's that, George?

GEORGE Keep away from Keeney.

BUTT What's wrong with Keeney?

GEORGE The governor has asked us to submit a report on your conduct here and in all honesty I can find nothing good to say about him. The rest of you — you did the job to the best of your ability, and I'll say that, and it'll be taken into consideration. But Keeney — a danger-man, Butt, a real danger-man. No loyalty to anyone or anything — that's his trouble. No loyalty to the job. I doubt very much if he's even loyal to what the rest of you stand for. But I'm telling you nothing new, Butt. You know. He's heading for disaster. Keep away from him. All right? (*Aloud again*) Better take my friend up to the office for safekeeping.

BUTT, *who is closer to the jug than George, stoops and lifts it.*

That's an example — you saw the way he was throwing that about. No appreciation whatever.

BUTT That's right.

GEORGE I was just saying to Dr. King last night: if we'd got nothing else here, the dig would have been worth it for that alone. Exquisite, isn't it?

BUTT Good.

GEORGE Really beautiful. (*Holds out his hand*) Thanks — I'll take it up.

> BUTT *has been staring at the jug since he lifted it off the ground. Now, without taking his eyes off it, he opens his hand and the jug falls on the ground and is smashed to pieces.*

GEORGE Oh my God — (*He drops on his knees*) Oh my God (*Gathering the pieces together, almost in tears*) — Damn you, Butt! God damn you to hell! Oh my God, you'll pay for this, Butt! By God you'll pay and pay and pay — I'll see to it that you pay! There'll be nothing in your life that you'll regret as much as this! I promise you, Butt — that's a promise! This'll be the biggest regret of your life! Oh my God, how you'll regret this!

> *He has gathered the pieces together and rushes off with them up the steps.* BUTT *looks after him with flat eyes. Then* KEENEY's *singing diverts him and he returns to his work.*

KEENEY (*Off*) Fare thee well, for I must leave thee;
Do not let this parting grieve thee.

> *He enters.*

And remember that the best of friends must part,
must part.

PYNE (*Entering from other side; he and* KEENEY *sing together*)

Adieu, adieu, kind friends, adieu, adieu, adieu.
I can no longer stay with you, stay with you.
(PYNE *continues whistling*)

KEENEY Well, there you are, Buttie Boy. We spend months and months making a bloody big hole and next week a different crowd of tribesmen'll come along and fill it all in. If a fella had any head on him at all, he'd be able to extract some kind of wisdom from that. Wouldn't he, Leif? Where did the jug go?

BUTT George took it up with him.

KEENEY You may be sure.

BUTT He's sending in a report about us to the governor.

KEENEY That'll be thrilling material.

PYNE I know what he'll say about me. 'Pyne is just . . . ' (*He closes his eyes, purses his lips, and makes a kissing sound quickly three times*) And Jesus, if word of that gets around, I'll never get a night's sleep.

SMILER *enters in his street clothes.*

KEENEY What'll he say about Butt?

PYNE Oh he respects Butt.

KEENEY 'The success of the venture was due in large measure to Butt whose brilliant wit, ready smile and endless good humour made the sometimes tedious work a constant pleasure.'

PYNE Bloody hell!

KEENEY 'He was an example to all of us. He is survived by a wife and ten children.'

PYNE Ha-ha. What'll he say about you? (*Calls*) Hi, George, are you going to give Keeney a good report?

KEENEY 'I found it difficult at first to get to know Keeney because of his natural reticence and his modest disposition. But when I got past that carefully cultivated armour of a shy man, I discovered a very real, a very warm human being. It was a privilege to know him.'

PYNE Ho-ho-ho. What about Knox?

KNOX *enters.*

KNOX What about Knox?

KEENEY 'Knox was our Adonis. His golden locks and blue eyes will haunt me till I die.'

KNOX Wilson's here. He's talking to someone up at the gate.

The announcement has the finality of a sentence. Pause.

PYNE So Wilson's here. Well. There you are — the end of the line. Wilson's here. Well, that's it, lads. Back to porridge.

SMILER Porridge — that's right, Pyne — that's right.

PYNE Bloody right, Smiler. And it'll be a hell of a relief to get peace from Keeney's yapping, won't it? Won't it, Knoxie?

Brief pause. Then sings:

Adieu, kind friends, adieu, adieu, adieu . . . (*The words fade. He whistles*)

BUTT (*To* KEENEY) About next Monday —

PYNE (*Very quickly, very sharply*) What about it?

BUTT This is our last chance to talk about it.

PYNE What's there to talk about?

BUTT As Knoxie says, maybe now that we're back with them, maybe there'll be no trouble — maybe the whole thing'll be dropped.

PYNE 'As Knoxie says' — Jesus sake you're really desperate if you're listening to bloody Knoxie! George is very quiet. (*Calls*) Working on your bloody report, George?

BUTT The question is — if they're going to go ahead — what's the best thing for us to do?

PYNE (*Bitterly, rapidly*) What d'you want us to do? Take Wilson aside when he comes in and say to him, 'Mr. Wilson, can you help us with our little problem? We understand that some of us are going to get killed in a riot next Monday night. What advice do you have to offer us, Mr. Wilson?' Jesus! You know what he'd say — Wilson — you know what he'd say? 'Fucking wonderful!' That's what he'd say. 'Pity there weren't fucking twenty of you!' That's what he'd say!

BUTT So we do nothing, Keeney — is that it?

PYNE What's your suggestion?

BUTT We could —

PYNE (*On the point of tears*) Fight them? Take them all on? Five of us against two hundred of them? That'd be some contest. Or what about throwing ourselves on the mercies of the authorities — plead for a transfer to the Curragh — there's only seventy of our old companions there. That'd be a more equal fight.

BUTT So we do nothing, Keeney? Is that it? We do nothing?

> *Pause. Then* KEENEY *begins very softly, very soberly, as if he were about to deliver a solution.*

KEENEY Listen to me, boys. Where we are now, this very spot we're standing on, this is going to be the foundation of an enormous glass and steel hotel with a swimming-pool in the basement and a restaurant on the roof. And to make that foundation is going to take hundreds and hundreds of tons of hard-core. And all that hard-core is going to come thundering down over the top there —

PYNE So what?

KEENEY — right down here — on top of old Leif. And my suggestion is —

PYNE Your suggestion is?

KEENEY My suggestion is that we should demonstrate our affection and our respect for our friend here by burying him properly now.

PYNE Jesus, Keeney. (*Meaning: Is there no limit to your fooling?*)

SMILER That's right, Keeney, that's right.

KEENEY Thank you Smiler. (*Moving* KNOX *aside*) I beg your pardon, Knox.

> KEENEY *opens up the tarpaulin and spreads it over the skeleton. Then he secures the sides and bottom with stones and pieces of timber. The skull is left exposed. While he is doing this job . . .*

KNOX (*To* BUTT) What does he think he's at?

KEENEY *now stands at the exposed skull.*

KEENEY I'm not a religious man myself. But if some of you would
like to . . . ? Pyne? Butt?

KNOX (*Privately to* BUTT) I hid your share in your boots.

KEENEY Knoxie? No? Well . . . (*He clears his throat; in the same
sober tones*) The last time I saw him — the first week of
last May as a matter of fact — he was talking and laughing and joking as usual — the old Leif we all remember
so well. But there was a definite something about him
that day — it was a Tuesday, I remember, a warm,
breathless day — an unrest, a disquiet — it's difficult to
define. And perhaps I'm investing that last meeting with
a significance it didn't in fact have. But he said
something that day that I think you ought to know.
(GEORGE *is now tidying up on the terrace*) He propped
himself up on his elbow — the conversation up to that
had been vintage Leif, the usual brilliant persiflage —
but he suddenly got up on his elbow and he gazed at me
for I'm sure thirty seconds with those extraordinary eyes
of his — remember those grey eyes? — and he said, 'Tell
me, George — ' 'It's Keeney, Leif,' I said. But he was so
intense he didn't hear me. 'Tell me, George,' he said, 'I
must know — I *must* know — was Hamlet really mad?'

PYNE Jesus! Hi, George!

GEORGE *goes into the office.*

KEENEY And then he collapsed. It was all over. (*No longer
solemn*) God rest you, me aul' buttie!

PYNE Me darlin' soldier laddie!

KEENEY Isn't he looking like himself, though?

PYNE The spitting image of himself.

KEENEY And content?

PYNE Lovely.

KEENEY And the wee smile on his lips.

PYNE Like a child, God be kind to him.

KEENEY One civil man, Leif.

PYNE   Never harmed man nor beast.

KEENEY   And generous — give you the shirt off his back.

PYNE   The bite out of his mouth.

KEENEY   One of nature's gentlemen.

PYNE   A great husband — a great father.

KEENEY   May the hard-core rest light on him.

PYNE   We'll never see his likes again.

KEENEY   All the same, boys —

PYNE   What?

KEENEY   Is there a look of the mother's side of the house about the set of that jaw?

PYNE   The Boyces of Ballybeg?

KEENEY   They all had that hard, jutting jaw.

PYNE   Now that you mention it.

KEENEY   Tight crowd, the Boyces.

PYNE   He favoured the mother's side all right.

KEENEY   Tight and bitter.

PYNE   And notionate, too.

KEENEY   Man, they held grudges for generations. And in drink —!

PYNE   Balubas!

KEENEY   Be Jaysus they'd fight with their shadow.

PYNE   And did, too.

KEENEY   Oh, he's a Boyce all right.

PYNE   One bad connection.

KEENEY   One hungry connection.

PYNE   Hungry's the word.

KEENEY   Hungry and vicious.

PYNE   Bad seed — bad breed.

KEENEY *briskly covers the skull with the tarpaulin.*

KEENEY   All our bad luck go with him.

PYNE   Amen to that.

WILSON *enters. He is in the uniform of a prison officer. His manner seems crisper and more officious now that he is in uniform.*

WILSON   Right — right — right — the holiday's over. Out you go and get changed. Look smart — make it snappy. Come

84

on, Smiler, put an inch to that step. Get a move on — we haven't all day. Move, Knox, move, move, move. Come on, Butt. Shift, Pyne, shift.

The diggers move off morosely.

Good evening, George.
GEORGE (*Coming down steps*) Good evening, Mr. Wilson.
WILSON Touch of frost again this evening.
GEORGE The winter's here, Mr. Wilson.
WILSON Would you think so?
GEORGE It's not far away, anyhow.
WILSON Well, we did all right, I suppose. (*Lowering voice*) By the way, George, she did great.
GEORGE Who?
WILSON Dolly.
GEORGE Oh, the exam. And she did well?
WILSON *Very* well.
GEORGE I'm glad of that, Mr. Wilson.
WILSON Very well indeed. I'm very satisfied.
GEORGE Naturally.
WILSON Hell of a nice chap — English — you know — no side with him — a man you could talk to.
GEORGE That was a help.
WILSON Said she played 'with grace and discretion'.
GEORGE Very nice.
WILSON I think that's encouraging.
GEORGE Certainly is.
WILSON You know — for a girl there. I mean when an expert like that says she plays with grace and discretion, George, it's no bad recommendation for a young slip of a girl — am I right?
GEORGE Indeed.
WILSON Playing a difficult instrument with grace and discretion, George, you would call that high praise, wouldn't you?
GEORGE It's all that.
WILSON Oh, she has grace all right — I can see that myself and I'm no musician. But what do you make of the discretion part? That doesn't make much sense to me, George.
GEORGE I think that's good, Mr. Wilson.

WILSON The wife thinks so, too. I hope you're right. 'With grace and discretion.' The grace — that's grand — that's all right.

GEORGE She must be a graceful player, Mr. Wilson.

WILSON Oh, lovely to look at, just lovely.

GEORGE And he spotted that — there you are.

WILSON He might have got a better bloody word than 'discretion'.

GEORGE I don't know, Mr. Wilson. Depends on how he said it.

WILSON 'Discretion' — in the name of God wasn't that a rotten thing to say about a wee girl trying to do her best? English expert my arse! He knows as much about it as I know myself!

Enter KEENEY *and* KNOX *in street clothes.*

KEENEY (*Very demurely*) We're ready when you are, Mr. Wilson.

WILSON Okay. Fine. Off we go.

GEORGE Mr. Wilson —

WILSON Yes, George?

GEORGE I want a word with you.

WILSON Now?

GEORGE No, no, not here; not now.

WILSON Are you sure?

GEORGE No, I'll call you later tonight.

Enter PYNE *and* BUTT.

WILSON Okay. (*To others*) All right — are we all set? Where's Smiler? (SMILER *enters*) Last as usual, Smiler.

SMILER That's right.

WILSON Up to the van then. Have you all your stuff with you?

BUTT It's up at the gate.

WILSON Good. Off we go. I'll be hearing from you, George?

GEORGE About nine o'clock tonight — will that suit?

WILSON Perfect. We're away then. Come on — come on — move — move.

He goes off. GEORGE *looks momentarily at the diggers and then busies himself picking up the tea things.*

BUTT Goodbye, George.
GEORGE (*Without looking up*) Bye.
BUTT Coming, Smiler?
SMILER Yes, Butt.
BUTT Will we sit at the front or the back?
SMILER I like the front.
BUTT That's where we'll sit then and we'll see all the sights.

BUTT *and* SMILER *exit.*

KEENEY (*To* KNOX) Say goodbye to George, Knoxie.

KNOX *shrugs his shoulders, grunts something and shuffles off.*

Actually he's heart-broken. A real aul' softie, Knox.
WILSON (*Off*) Come on! Come on!
KEENEY What does he want?
PYNE He wants us to go with him.
KEENEY Why?
PYNE Because he *likes* us.
KEENEY Does he?
PYNE He does — genuinely.
KEENEY Why couldn't he say that to our faces?
PYNE He's shy, like George.
KEENEY Will we go with him?
PYNE I'm easy. Maybe we should.
KEENEY Okay. Maybe he needs us more than George. (*To* GEORGE) It has been a *great* pleasure, George; and I would like to think that fate will bring us together again some day. (*To* PYNE) Do you think it will?
PYNE With the help of God.
KEENEY You know, he really expanded my horizons.
PYNE Sure that's his trade.
KEENEY Did he expand your horizons?
PYNE He tried hard but mine were seized up with the frost.
KEENEY Well, mine he expanded and expanded and expanded until I thought, honest to God, they'd just snap.
PYNE But they didn't.
KEENEY They did not, more power to him.

WILSON *(Off)* Keeney! Pyne!

PYNE Like a spoiled child, isn't he? George, don't move, George, I want to remember you as you are now. (*Blows a kiss*) Au revoir, my love.

He goes. Pause.

KEENEY What can I say, George, that won't sound trite? Friend, good friend, site-manager — may God take care of you.

He goes. Now that everyone is gone, GEORGE stops working, straightens up, and looks after them. Pause. Suddenly KEENEY's head appears.

On an archaeological site
Five diggers examined their plight
But a kangaroo court
Gave the final report —

WILSON *(Off)* Keeney!

KEENEY They were only a parcel of . . .

Good night, sweet prince.

He disappears again. Pause. Then GEORGE goes to Leif's grave, kicks away the stones and timbers, then pulls off the tarpaulin, and begins folding it. As he does this, bring the lights down slowly.